Is That Correct?— Checking Math Problems

Grade 3

Published by Instructional Fair
an imprint of

McGraw Hill Children's Publishing

Editors: Melissa Warner Hale, Krista Fanning

McGraw Hill Children's Publishing

Published by Instructional Fair
An imprint of McGraw-Hill Children's Publishing
Copyright © 2004 McGraw-Hill Children's Publishing

All Rights Reserved • Printed in the United States of America

Limited Reproduction Permission: Permission to duplicate these materials is limited to the person for whom they are purchased. Reproduction for an entire school or school district is unlawful and strictly prohibited.

Send all inquiries to:
McGraw-Hill Children's Publishing
3195 Wilson Drive NW
Grand Rapids, Michigan 49544

Is That Correct?—Checking Math Problems—grade 3
ISBN: 0-7424-2783-8

1 2 3 4 5 6 7 8 9 MAL 09 08 07 06 05 04

The *McGraw·Hill* Companies

Table Of Contents

Introduction 4

Number and Operations
Rounding Numbers 5
Composing Numbers 6
Decomposing Numbers 7
Comparing Whole Numbers 8-9
Comparing Decimals 10-11
Ordering Whole Numbers 12
Ordering Decimals 13
Parts of a Whole 14-15
Parts of a Set 16-17
Comparing Fractions 18-19
Equivalent Fractions 20-21
Adding Fractions 22
Subtracting Fractions 23
Adding Whole Numbers 24-27
Subtracting Whole Numbers 28-31
Mixed Addition and Subtraction 32-33
Adding and Subtracting Decimals 34-35
Multiplication 36-39
Division 40-43
Multiplication and Division 44-45
Riddles 46
Applications—Addition and Subtraction 47-48
Applications—Multiplication 49
Applications—Division 50
Applications—Multiplication and Division 51

Algebra
Patterns 52-54
Commutative Property 55
Associative Property 56-57
Function Tables 58-59
Variables 60-63
Applications—Writing Equations 64-67
Applications—Graphing 68-69

Geometry
Similar and Congruent 70-71
Symmetry 72-73
Reflections and Rotations 74-75
Types of Triangles 76-77
Polygons 78-79
3-Dimensional Shapes 80-81
Applications—Point of View 82
Applications—Nets 83
Applications—Using a Grid 84-85
Applications—Coordinate Graphing 86-87

Measurement
Area and Perimeter 88-89
Volume 90-91
Customary Units 92-93
Metric Units 94-95
Converting Customary Lengths 96-97
Converting Metric Lengths 98-99
Applications—Money 100-101
Applications—Time 102-103
Applications—Temperature 104-105

Data Analysis and Probability
How Likely? 106
Equally Likely? 107-108
Probability 109-111
Range 112
Mode 113
Median 114
Mean 115
Applications—Interpreting Data 116-117
Applications—Tally Charts 118-119
Applications—Line Plots 120
Applications—Bar Graphs 121-122

Answer Key 123-128

Introduction

Is That Correct?—Checking Math Problems provides many opportunities for students to sharpen their analytical and self-assessment abilities. Students will learn to recognize and correct the common errors associated with a particular skill and become proficient at using answer-checking techniques that are adaptable to any mathematical or problem-solving situation. All this is done in the context of practicing essential math skills.

This book is organized according to the content standards set forth by the National Council of Teachers of Mathematics. A mix of grade-appropriate skill-practice and problem-solving activities are included from each content standard—Number and Operations, Algebra, Geometry, Measurement, and Data Analysis and Probability. The guided questioning format incorporates the NCTM process standards of Problem Solving, Reasoning and Proof, Connections, Representation, and Communication.

Guided activities teach students how to analyze sample student answers. The analysis is broken down into two essential components—Is That Correct? and Check Your Work. First, students learn how to use estimation, work a problem backwards, or put the answer back into the problem to determine whether or not an answer makes sense. Next, they learn many different tools—such as carefully examining each step, solving problems using another strategy, or using a model—for finding and correcting errors.

Finally, students get a chance to practice the skills they have learned on similar problems. Students perform the computations and then use the new techniques to check their own work. Scattered throughout the book are Error Alert! indicators that provide pointers and tips for avoiding common mistakes.

Name _____ Date _____

<Number and Operations>

Rounding Numbers

Error Alert! Look at the digit to the right of the place value to which you are rounding. If the digit is 5 or more, round up. If the digit is less than 5, round down.

Problem: Round each number to the nearest ten.

    A. 216   **B.** 132   **C.** 558   **D.** 675

Becky's Answers:

A. 200 **B.** 100 **C.** 600 **D.** 700

Mary's Answers:

A. 210 **B.** 130 **C.** 550 **D.** 670

Is That Correct?—Does the answer match the question?

1. Look at Becky's answers. She rounded to the nearest _____. The directions said to round each number to the nearest _____. Did Becky follow the directions? _____ Are her answers correct? _____

2. Look at Mary's answers. Did she round her values to the correct place value? _____ Did she round the values correctly? Explain.

3. Write the correct answer to each problem.

    A. _____ **B.** _____ **C.** _____ **D.** _____

Practice

Round each number to the nearest hundred. Then check your work.

4. 921 _____ **5.** 662 _____ **6.** 1,882 _____ **7.** 21,473 _____

© McGraw-Hill Children's Publishing   0-7424-2783-8 *Is That Correct?*

Name _____ Date _____

(Number and Operations)

Composing Numbers

Problem: Write this number in standard form: 10,000 + 400 + 60 + 8

Jerome's Answer: 1,468   **Darnel's Answer:** 14,068

Is That Correct?—Does the answer make sense?

1. Should the answer be more or less than 10,000? How do you know?

2. Whose answer is obviously wrong? What mistake do you think he made?

Check Your Work—Compare the answer to the original problem.

3. Check Darnel's answer. Look at each digit. Name the amount each digit represents. Does Darnel's answer match the original problem?

   <u>1</u>4,068 = one ten thousand = 10,000
   1<u>4</u>,068 = _____ thousands = _____
   14,<u>0</u>68 = _____ = _____
   14,0<u>6</u>8 = _____ = _____
   14,06<u>8</u> = _____ = _____

4. Write the correct answer: _____
   What did Darnel do wrong?

Practice

Write the standard form for each number. Then check your work.

5. 400,000 + 20,000 + 1,000 + 20 + 6 = _____
6. 300,000 + 200 + 70 + 8 = _____

Error Alert! If there is no number for a particular place value, remember to put a zero in that spot.

Name _____ Date _____

<Number and Operations>

Decomposing Numbers

Problem: Write the number 12,507 in expanded form.

Deshawna's Answer: 1,000 + 200 + 50 + 7
Jamila's Answer: 10,000 + 200 + 50 + 7
Kineisha's Answer: 10,000 + 2,000 + 500 + 7
Lavonn's Answer: 10,000 + 2,000 + 50 + 7
Ronelle's Answer: 10,000 + 2,000 + 500 + 70

Is That Correct?—Does the answer make sense?

1. Whose answer is obviously wrong? _____ Why?

Check Your Work—Work the problem backwards.

2. Check Ronelle's answer by adding. Does her answer match the original problem?

    10,000
     2,000
       500
    + 70
    _____

3. Check the other students' answers on another piece of paper. Did anyone get the problem right? Who?

Practice

Write each number in expanded form. When finished, compare your answers with a classmate. Decide on the correct answers.

4. 7,216 _____

5. 204,125 _____

6. 616,000 _____

Name _____   Date _____

(Number and Operations)

Comparing Whole Numbers

Error Alert! The > and < signs point to the smaller number. Make sure the arrow points to the smallest number. Both 3 < 7 (3 is less than 7) and 7 > 3 (7 is greater than 3) are correct.

Problems: Place the correct symbol (< or >) between each pair of numbers.

Lashawn's Answers:

1. 2,219 > 2,125
2. 67 < 76
3. 4,011 > 4,110
4. 575 < 755
5. 463 > 453
6. 94 < 93
7. 132 > 213
8. 54 < 74
9. 1,002 < 1,012

✓ Check Your Work—Make a model

Use base-ten blocks to build each pair of numbers. Which number is the smallest? Does the sign (< or >) point to the smallest number? Circle each wrong answer.

Example:

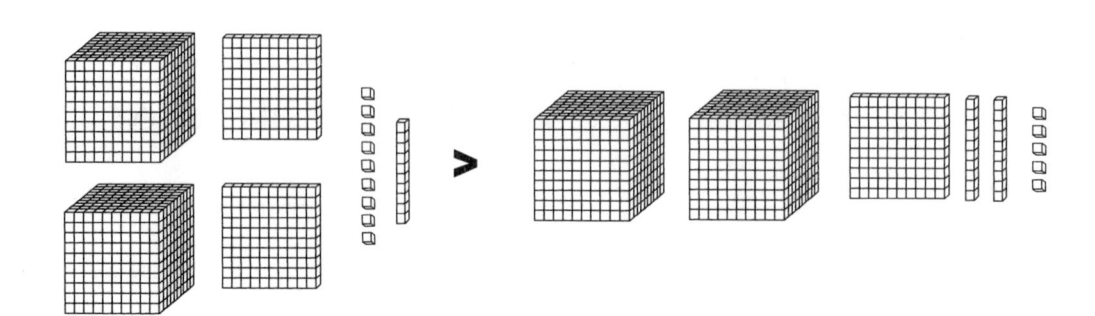

© McGraw-Hill Children's Publishing

0-7424-2783-8 *Is That Correct?*

Name _____   Date _____

<Number and Operations>

Comparing Whole Numbers

Practice

Place the correct symbol (< or >) between each pair of numbers.

1. 36 < 82
2. 4,627 < 4,672
3. 74 > 47
4. 4,882 > 4,890
5. 7 < 11
6. 5,019 > 5,009
7. 77 > 17
8. 4,657 > 4,567

9. 23 < 72
10. 2,034 > 1,299
11. 572 > 527
12. 12,536 < 21,536
13. 362 > 189
14. 52,218 < 78,000
15. 921 > 912
16. 37,151 > 15,137

Check Your Work

Look at each pair of numbers one digit at a time from left to right. Compare the digits at each place value. Which is more? That number is higher. If the digits are the same, move to the next place value.

Example: How does 4,627 compare to 4,672?

<u>4</u>,627 ? <u>4</u>,672	4 thousands = 4 thousands	Keep going.
4,<u>6</u>27 ? 4,<u>6</u>72	6 hundreds = 6 hundreds	Keep going.
4,6<u>2</u>7 ? 4,6<u>7</u>2	2 tens < 7 tens	

So 4,627 < 4,672

Check all your answers. Write the corrections next to the problem. Be prepared to explain why you changed your answer.

Name _____   Date _____

(Number and Operations)

Comparing Decimals

Error Alert! The > and < signs point to the smaller number. Make sure the arrow points to the smallest number. Both 4.3 < 4.7 (4.3 is less than 4.7) and 4.7 > 4.3 (4.7 is greater than 4.3) are correct.

Problems: Place the correct symbol (< or >) between each pair of numbers.

Melissa's Answers:

1. 3.21 > 2.12
2. 2.67 < 2.62
3. 4.5 > 3.9
4. 5.7 < 7.5
5. 4.63 > 4.53
6. 0.76 < 0.66
7. 3.09 < 3.90
8. 8.2 < 9.4
9. 2.1 < 2.9

Check Your Work

Check Melissa's work. Look at each pair of numbers one digit at a time from left to right. Compare the digits that are at the same place values. Which is more? That number is higher. If the digits are the same, check the next place value. Circle any wrong answers.

Example:

Is 2.67 < 2.62?

<u>2</u>.67 ? <u>2</u>.62   2 ones = 2 ones
                        check the next place value

2.<u>6</u>7 ? 2.<u>6</u>2   6 tenths = 6 tenths
                        check the next place value

2.6<u>7</u> ? 2.6<u>2</u>   7 hundredths > 2 hundredths
2.67 > 2.62

Is 2.67 < 2.62?   No. Melissa's answer is incorrect.

Name _____ Date _____

<Number and Operations>

Comparing Decimals

Error Alert! If two numbers do not have the same number of places after the decimal, add zero(s) to the end of a number to make them the same. Then compare the digits.

Example: 3.6 ? 3.65 ⟶ 3.60 < 3.65

Practice

Place the correct symbol (<, >, or =) between each pair of numbers.

1. 3.6 ☐ 8.2
2. 4.62 ☐ 4.67
3. 7.4 ☐ 4.7
4. 4.8 ☐ 4.89
5. 7 ☐ 7.1
6. 5.9 ☐ 5.09
7. 0.77 ☐ 1.7
8. 0.65 ☐ 0.567

9. 5.72 ☐ 5.27
10. 1.25 ☐ 1.53
11. 3.2 ☐ 3.18
12. 2.18 ☐ 2.28
13. 9.21 ☐ 9.12
14. 3.7 ☐ 3.70
15. 2.98 ☐ 2.9
16. 28.29 ☐ 8.92

Check Your Work

Check all your answers. Circle any wrong answers. Write the correct answer next to the problem. Be prepared to explain why you changed your answer.

© McGraw-Hill Children's Publishing   0-7424-2783-8 *Is That Correct?*

Name _____ Date _____

(Number and Operations)

Ordering Whole Numbers

Problem: Put the following numbers in order from least to greatest.

2,451   2,405   2,045   2,415   2,514   2,541

Ashley's Answer: 2,045   2,405   2,514   2,415   2,541   2,451
Madison's Answer: 2,541   2,514   2,451   2,415   2,405   2,045

Is That Correct?—Does the answer match the question?

1. Read the directions carefully. Then look at Madison's answer. What mistake did she make?

2. Check Ashley's answer. Is it correct? _____ How do you know?

3. Write the correct answer. _____

Error Alert! Is the order correct? Look at only two numbers at a time. Is the first number smaller than the second? If not, then the numbers are out of order. If so, compare the second and third numbers, then the third and fourth numbers, and so on.

Practice

Place each set of numbers in order from least to greatest.

4. 789 800 799 1,000 678 798 _____

5. 1,203   1,032   1,320   1,204   1,432   1,023

6. 24,712   21,471   27,412   24,127   21,417   27,214

Check Your Work

Trade papers with a classmate. Compare your answers.

© McGraw-Hill Children's Publishing   0-7424-2783-8 *Is That Correct?*

Name _____ Date _____

<Number and Operations>

Ordering Decimals

Problem: Put the following numbers in order from least to greatest.
   5.4   4.9   5.49   6.2   4.61   6.12

José's Answer: 4.9   4.61   5.4   5.49   6.2   6.12
Juan's Answer: 6.12   6.2   5.4   5.49   4.61   4.9

✓ Check Your Work

José explains how he got his answers.

"First, I looked at the number in front of the decimal. Four goes before 5, and 5 goes before 6. Then, I counted the place values to the right of the decimal. If there's only 1 place value, then that's smaller than having 2 place values. So 4.9 is smaller than 4.61 and 5.4 is smaller than 5.49."

Juan explains how he got his answers.

"Some of the numbers had two digits after the decimal. Some only had one digit. I added a zero to the end of the numbers that only had one digit after the decimal. Then I compared the numbers after the decimals. So, if you compare 5.49 to 5.40, you can see that 40 is smaller than 49, so 5.40 comes before 5.49."

1. On another piece of paper, explain what is wrong with José's reasoning.

2. Is Juan's statement correct? _____

3. Look at the first digit in each number from Juan's answer. Is his answer correct? _____ What did Juan forget to do?

4. Explain how to find the correct answer. You may want to use ideas from both José and Juan. Write the correct answer to the problem.

Name _____ Date _____

(Number and Operations)

Parts of a Whole

Problem: Write the fraction for the shaded part of each figure.

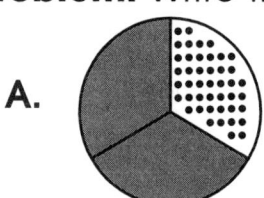

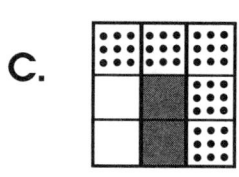

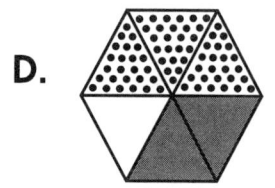

A.   B.   C.   D.

Cho's Answers: A. $\frac{3}{2}$ B. $\frac{4}{1}$ C. $\frac{9}{2}$ D. $\frac{6}{2}$ **Kwan's Answers:** A. $\frac{1}{3}$ B. $\frac{2}{4}$ C. $\frac{5}{9}$ D. $\frac{3}{6}$

Error Alert! The denominator (bottom number) of a fraction tells how many equal parts a shape is divided into. The numerator (top number) of a fraction tells how many parts are selected for a characteristic.

shaded = $\frac{4}{8}$, dotted = $\frac{1}{8}$, white = $\frac{3}{8}$

Is That Correct?—Does the answer match the question?

1. Look at Cho's answers. Are they correct? _____

2. What mistake did Cho make?

3. Look at Kwan's answers. Do her fractions represent the **shaded** part of each figure? _____

4. What do Kwan's answers represent?

5. Write the correct fraction for the shaded part of each figure above.

   A. _____   B. _____   C. _____   D. _____

© McGraw-Hill Children's Publishing

0-7424-2783-8 *Is That Correct?*

Name _____ Date _____

<Number and Operations>

Parts of a Whole

Practice

Write the fraction that represents the chosen part of each figure.

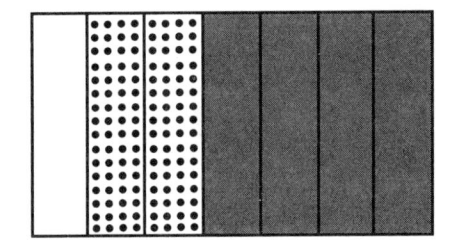

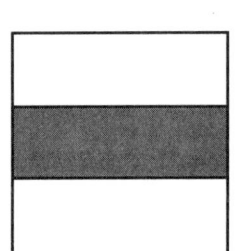

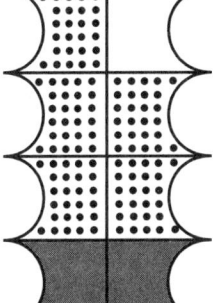

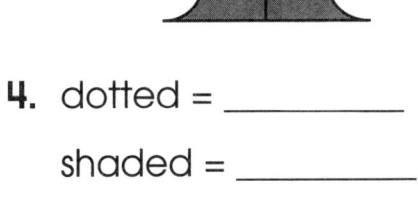

1. dotted = _____
   shaded = _____
   white = _____

2. dotted = _____
   shaded = _____
   white = _____

3. dotted = _____
   shaded = _____
   white = _____

4. dotted = _____
   shaded = _____
   white = _____

Check Your Work

Check each fraction. Does the denominator show how many total parts? Does the numerator show how many parts are shaded, dotted, or white?

© McGraw-Hill Children's Publishing

0-7424-2783-8 *Is That Correct?*

Name _____   Date _____

(Number and Operations)

Parts of a Set

Error Alert! The denominator (bottom number) of a fraction tells how many objects are in the set. The numerator (top number) a fraction tells how many objects have that trait.

Problem: What fraction of the vases is broken?

Davonn's Answer: $\frac{4}{2}$

Jamal's Answer: $\frac{2}{6}$

Lamarr's Answer: $\frac{4}{6}$

Keishawn's Answer: $\frac{4}{2}$

Is That Correct?—Know the correct definitions.

1. How do you think Davonn got his answer? What would you tell Davonn?

2. How do you think Keishawn got his answer? What would you tell Keishawn?

3. Which students used the correct number in the denominator?

4. Look at the numerators these students used. Which one is correct?

5. What did the student who made a mistake do wrong?

© McGraw-Hill Children's Publishing

0-7424-2783-8 *Is That Correct?*

Name _____ Date _____

<Number and Operations>

PARTS OF A SET

PRACTICE

Write the fraction that represents the chosen trait.

1. growling dogs: _____

2. crying babies: _____

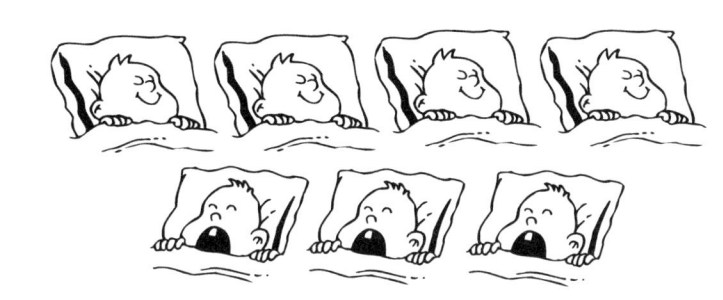

3. dropped cones: _____

4. live flowers: _____

5. rotten apples: _____

Check Your Work

Justify your answers. Explain to a friend what the numerator and denominator of each fraction means.

Name _____ Date _____

(Number and Operations)

COMPARING FRACTIONS

Problems: Which fraction is larger? Place the correct sign (< or >) between each pair of fractions.

Brianna's Answers:

1. $\frac{2}{5} < \frac{7}{8}$

2. $\frac{1}{4} > \frac{2}{3}$

3. $\frac{4}{6} < \frac{1}{5}$

4. $\frac{8}{9} > \frac{4}{8}$

5. $\frac{1}{3} > \frac{3}{4}$

6. $\frac{4}{7} < \frac{5}{6}$

7. $\frac{3}{4} > \frac{1}{2}$

8. $\frac{1}{2} < \frac{7}{8}$

9. $\frac{4}{5} < \frac{4}{6}$

10. $\frac{3}{10} < \frac{2}{5}$

11. $\frac{5}{6} < \frac{1}{3}$

12. $\frac{2}{4} > \frac{5}{8}$

✓ Check Your Work—Use a model.

On another piece of paper, use a compass to draw 12 pairs of circles. Make each circle exactly the same size. For each problem, draw a model of each fraction and shade the correct number of parts. Make sure the sign (< or >) points to the fraction with the smallest portion of the circle shaded. Circle each answer of Brianna's that is wrong.

Name _____ Date _____

<Number and Operations>

COMPARING FRACTIONS

ERROR ALERT! Think about what the fraction means. The denominator tells into how many parts something is divided. The numerator tells how many parts are chosen.

Which piece of the pie would you rather eat?

$\frac{1}{2}$ = 1 part of out 2 equal parts $\frac{1}{4}$ = 1 part out of 4 equal parts

Practice

Which fraction is larger? Place the correct sign (< or >) between each pair of fractions.

1. $\frac{2}{3}$ ☐ $\frac{1}{3}$ 2. $\frac{1}{4}$ ☐ $\frac{5}{8}$ 3. $\frac{3}{6}$ ☐ $\frac{1}{4}$

4. $\frac{4}{9}$ ☐ $\frac{2}{3}$ 5. $\frac{1}{4}$ ☐ $\frac{4}{5}$ 6. $\frac{3}{6}$ ☐ $\frac{1}{4}$

7. $\frac{1}{3}$ ☐ $\frac{7}{8}$ 8. $\frac{7}{9}$ ☐ $\frac{2}{7}$ 9. $\frac{1}{4}$ ☐ $\frac{1}{3}$

Check Your Work

Compare answers with a classmate. If any of your answers are different, draw a model to check. Decide whose answer is right. Be prepared to explain your answers.

Name _____ Date _____

(Number and Operations)

Equivalent Fractions

Problems: Write the missing numbers to make equivalent fractions.

A. $\frac{2}{4} = \frac{}{8}$ B. $\frac{1}{3} = \frac{}{6}$ C. $\frac{1}{3} = \frac{}{9}$

Justin's Answers: A. $\frac{2}{4} = \frac{6}{8}$ B. $\frac{1}{3} = \frac{4}{6}$ C. $\frac{1}{3} = \frac{7}{9}$

David's Answers: A. $\frac{2}{4} = \frac{4}{8}$ B. $\frac{1}{3} = \frac{2}{6}$ C. $\frac{1}{3} = \frac{3}{9}$

Is That Correct?—Does the answer match the question?

Every fraction has a decimal value. Use a calculator to find the decimal value of each fraction. Divide the numerator by the denominator.

1. Does each of Justin's fraction pairs have the same decimal value? _____ Does each of David's fraction pairs have the same decimal value? _____

   Justin showed his work for problem **A** like this: $\frac{2}{4} = \frac{2+4}{4+4} = \frac{6}{8}$

2. Why doesn't Justin's method work?

   David showed his work for problem **A** like this:

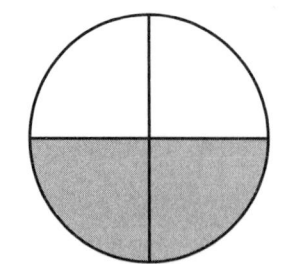

   $\frac{2}{4} = \frac{4}{8}$

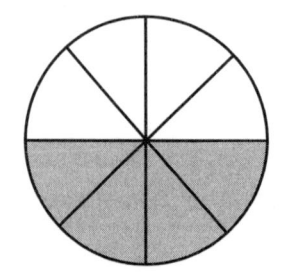

3. Check David's answers to **B** and **C**. Use the back of this page to draw models. Are his answers correct? _____

Name _____   Date _____

<Number and Operations>

Equivalent Fractions

PRACTICE

Write the missing numbers to make equivalent fractions. Shade the models to show that your answer is correct.

1. $\frac{1}{2} = \frac{}{4}$

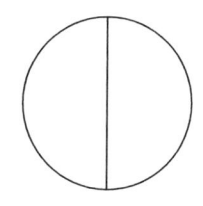

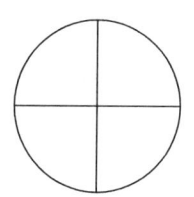

2. $\frac{1}{2} = \frac{}{8}$

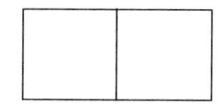

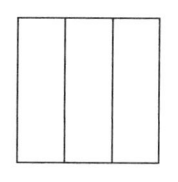

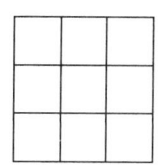

3. $\frac{2}{3} = \frac{}{9}$

4. $\frac{3}{4} = \frac{}{8}$

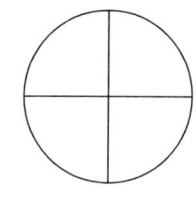

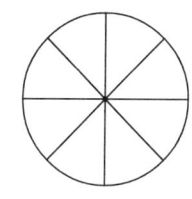

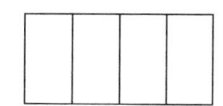

5. $\frac{1}{4} = \frac{}{12}$

6. $\frac{1}{2} = \frac{}{6}$

Is That Correct?—Does the answer match the question?

Compare your answers with a classmate. Discuss and correct any differences.

© McGraw-Hill Children's Publishing   0-7424-2783-8 Is That Correct?

Name _____ Date _____

(Number and Operations)

Adding Fractions

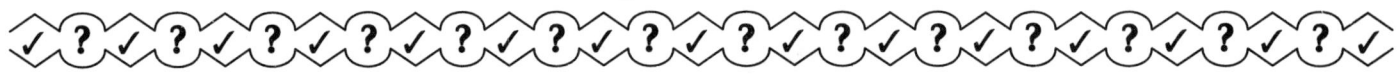

Problem: Add the fractions.
white and dotted = $\frac{1}{3} + \frac{1}{3}$ = ?

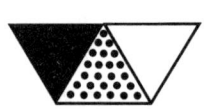

Chantara's Answer: $\frac{1}{3} + \frac{1}{3} = \frac{2}{6}$

Is That Correct?—Does the answer make sense?

1. How many total parts are in the diagram? _____ How many of those parts are shaded or dotted? _____ What fraction shows this? _____

2. Does Chantara's answer match the diagram? _____

3. Chantara didn't think about the diagram. She just added the numerators and denominators together. Explain how to add fractions correctly.

Practice

Add the fractions.

4. $\frac{1}{4} + \frac{2}{4}$ = _____   striped + white

5. $\frac{2}{5} + \frac{1}{5}$ = _____   black + white

6. $\frac{4}{8} + \frac{1}{8}$ = _____   striped + dotted

Check Your Work

Check to see if your answers make sense by comparing them to the models.

© McGraw-Hill Children's Publishing   0-7424-2783-8 Is That Correct?

Name _____ Date _____

<Number and Operations>

Subtracting Fractions

Problems: Subtract the fractions.

Antonio's Answers:

1. $\frac{3}{4} - \frac{2}{4} = \frac{1}{4}$

2. $\frac{4}{5} - \frac{1}{5} = \frac{5}{5}$

3. $\frac{8}{9} - \frac{6}{9} = \frac{2}{9}$

4. $\frac{4}{4} - \frac{2}{4} = \frac{6}{4}$

5. $\frac{9}{11} - \frac{4}{11} = \frac{4}{11}$

6. $\frac{6}{7} - \frac{4}{7} = \frac{2}{7}$

7. $\frac{5}{11} - \frac{1}{11} = \frac{6}{11}$

8. $\frac{5}{8} - \frac{3}{8} = \frac{2}{8}$

? Is That Correct?—Work the problem backwards.

Check each answer by using the inverse operation. Put a checkmark next to each wrong answer.

Example: Does $\frac{3}{4} - \frac{2}{4} = \frac{1}{4}$?

Yes, since $\frac{1}{4} + \frac{2}{4} = \frac{3}{4}$.

✓ Check Your Work—Look the answer over carefully.

Look at Antonio's wrong answers carefully. Did he perform the right operation (subtraction)? Did he remember to keep the denominators the same? Did he subtract the numerators correctly?

Correct Antonio's mistakes. Write the correct answer next to the problem. Be prepared to explain what mistake he made and how you fixed it.

© McGraw-Hill Children's Publishing   0-7424-2783-8 *Is That Correct?*

Name _____ Date _____
(Number and Operations)

Adding Whole Numbers

Problem: Find the sum.   **Shakeia's Answer:**
$$\begin{array}{r}256\\+\ 135\\\hline 381\end{array}$$

Is That Correct?—Use a model.

1. Here is a base-ten model of the problem. Compare the model to Shakeia's answer. Was she correct? _____

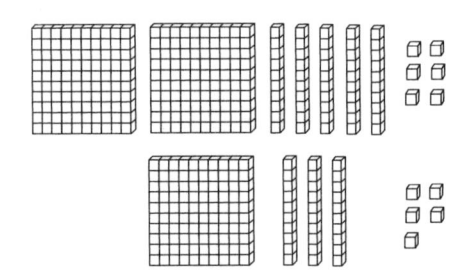

$$\begin{array}{r}256\\+\ 135\\\hline 381\end{array}$$

2. Look at Shakeia's work. What mistake did she make?

Practice

Find the sums.

3. $\begin{array}{r}148\\+\ 225\\\hline\end{array}$ 4. $\begin{array}{r}462\\+\ 371\\\hline\end{array}$ 5. $\begin{array}{r}559\\+\ 178\\\hline\end{array}$

Check Your Work

Build a base-ten model for each problem to check your work. Then look over each wrong answer to find your mistake.

Error Alert! If two digits have a sum greater than 10, don't forget to carry the tens digit!

Name _____ Date _____

<Number and Operations>

Adding Whole Numbers

Problem: Find the sum.   **Trayvon's Answer:**
```
   566
 + 295
 -----
   761
```

Is That Correct?—Use estimation.

1. Check Trayvon's answer. Round each addend to the nearest ten. Use mental math to add the rounded numbers. How does your answer compare to Trayvon's? Do you think his answer is correct? Why or why not?

2. Correct Trayvon's work. What mistake did he make?

Practice

Find the sums.

3.   864
   + 249

4.   567
   + 256

5.   173
   + 338

Check Your Work

Round each problem to the nearest ten to check your work. Put a checkmark next to wrong answers. Look over each wrong answer to find your mistake.

Error Alert! If two digits have a sum greater than 10, don't forget to carry the tens digit!

Name _____ Date _____

(Number and Operations)

Adding Whole Numbers

Problem: Find the sum.   **Michelle's Answer:**
$$\begin{array}{r}4,679\\+\ 3,371\\\hline 8,050\end{array}$$

Check Your Work—Use another strategy.

1. Jennifer checked Michelle's answer by pulling apart each number and then adding like numbers. Then she added the results to get the answer. Finish Jennifer's work.

2. Does Jennifer's answer match Michelle's? _____

$$4,679 = 4,000\ +\ 600\ +\ 70\ +\ 9$$

$$+\ 3,371 = 3,000\ +\ \underline{\quad}\ +\ \underline{\quad}\ +\ \underline{\quad}$$

$$7,000\ +\ \underline{\quad}\ +\ \underline{\quad}\ +\ \underline{\quad}\ =\ \underline{\quad\quad\quad}$$

Practice

Find the sums.

3. 5,323   4. 2,754   5. 5,693   6. 6,728
  + 2,417   + 1,459   + 1,046   + 2,193

Check Your Work

Check your answers using Jennifer's pull-apart strategy.

Name _____ Date _____

<Number and Operations>

Adding Whole Numbers

Practice

Find the sums.

1. 216
  + 425

  641

2. 627
  + 109

  736

3. 354
  + 617

  971

4. 648
  + 156

  804

5. 549
  + 157

  706

6. 438
  + 572

  1,010

7. 526
  + 248

  774

8. 357
  + 127

  484

9. 375
  + 162

  537

10. 3,583
   + 2,608

   6,191

11. 1,792
   + 4,526

   6,318

12. 5,731
   + 1,883

   7,614

Check Your Work

Use any method to check your work. Be prepared to explain how you know your answers are correct.

Name _____   Date _____

(Number and Operations)

Subtracting Whole Numbers

Problem: Find the difference.

Jorgé's Answer:
```
  72
- 45
----
  33
```

? Is That Correct?—Does the answer match the question?

Miguel checked Jorgé's answer using a base-ten model.

He drew blocks to represent 72:

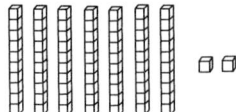

Then he circled the blocks that show 45.

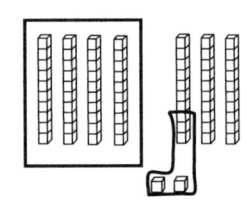

1. How many blocks does Miguel have left? _____ How does this answer compare to Jorgé's?

2. What mistake did Jorgé make?

Practice

Find the differences.

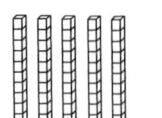

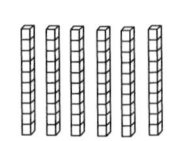

3.   56
   − 29
   ─────

4.   60
   − 43
   ─────

✓ Check Your Work

Use base-ten models to check your answers. For wrong answers, try to find your arithmetic mistake.

Name _____ Date _____

<Number and Operations>

Subtracting Whole Numbers

Problem: Find the difference.

Leticia's Answer:
```
   9
  5̶0̷2
-  114
  448
```

Error Alert: Check to make sure borrowing is done correctly.

Is That Correct?—Use estimation.

1. Check Leticia's answer. Round each number to the nearest hundred. Use mental math to subtract the rounded numbers. How does your answer compare to Leticia's? Do you think her answer is correct? Why or why not?

2. Look at Leticia's work. What mistake did she make?

Practice

Find the differences.

3.   440
   − 218
   ─────

4.   980
   − 309
   ─────

5.   530
   − 427
   ─────

Check Your Work

Check your answers by estimation. Round each number to the nearest hundred and subtract using mental arithmetic. Put a checkmark next to answers that aren't close to the estimate. Look at these answers carefully for mistakes.

© McGraw-Hill Children's Publishing   0-7424-2783-8 *Is That Correct?*

Name _____ Date _____

(Number and Operations)

Subtracting Whole Numbers

Problem: Find the difference. **Austin's Answer:**
$$\begin{array}{r} 2{,}562 \\ -\ 1{,}143 \\ \hline 1{,}419 \end{array}$$

✓ Check Your Work—Work the problem backwards.

1. Kevin checked Austin's work by using the inverse operation. Finish Kevin's work.

$$\begin{array}{r} 1{,}419 \\ +\ 1{,}143 \\ \hline \end{array}$$

2. Was Austin's answer correct? _____ How do you know?

⊙ Practice

Find the differences.

3. $\begin{array}{r} 5{,}323 \\ -\ 2{,}417 \\ \hline \end{array}$ 4. $\begin{array}{r} 2{,}754 \\ -\ 1{,}459 \\ \hline \end{array}$ 5. $\begin{array}{r} 6{,}274 \\ -\ 5{,}183 \\ \hline \end{array}$

6. $\begin{array}{r} 7{,}524 \\ -\ 3{,}257 \\ \hline \end{array}$ 7. $\begin{array}{r} 4{,}232 \\ -\ 2{,}038 \\ \hline \end{array}$ 8. $\begin{array}{r} 8{,}285 \\ -\ 6{,}715 \\ \hline \end{array}$

✓ Check Your Work

Check your answers by using the inverse operation.

Name _____ Date _____

<Number and Operations>

Subtracting Whole Numbers

Practice

Find the differences.

1. 732
   − 248
   _____

2. 512
   − 157
   _____

3. 842
   − 553
   _____

4. 765
   − 186
   _____

5. 540
   − 268
   _____

6. 829
   − 541
   _____

7. 423
   − 154
   _____

8. 600
   − 243
   _____

9. 642
   − 236
   _____

Check Your Work

Use any method to check your work. Be prepared to explain how you know your answers are correct.

© McGraw-Hill Children's Publishing

0-7424-2783-8 *Is That Correct?*

Name _____ Date _____

(Number and Operations)

Mixed Addition and Subtraction

Practice

Solve the addition and subtraction problems.

1. 345
  + 275

2. 197
  + 324

3. 783
  − 277

4. 165
  + 149

5. 903
  − 364

6. 255
  − 119

7. 712
  − 458

8. 263
  + 217

9. 521
  − 270

Check Your Work

Check each answer by working the problem backwards. Use the inverse (or opposite) operation.

Name _____ Date _____

<Number and Operations>

Mixed Addition and Subtraction

Practice

Solve the addition and subtraction problems.

1. 723
   − 116

2. 457
   + 325

3. 126
   + 327

4. 842
   − 628

5. 650
   − 444

6. 7,934
   − 4,746

7. 2,448
   + 2,739

8. 9,734
   − 4,841

9. 5,466
   + 7,523

Check Your Work

Use any method to check your answers. Use a model, estimate, perform the inverse operation, or use the pull-apart method.

Name _____ Date _____

(Number and Operations)

Adding and Subtracting Decimals

Problems: Solve each addition and subtraction problem.

Aleita's Answers:

1. 4.2 − 3.9 = 3
2. 5.61 − 2.7 = 2.91
3. 8.1 − 5.3 = 2.8
4. 12.5 + 4.21 = 5.46
5. 3.3 + 5.8 = 9.1
6. 7.13 − 6.29 = 84
7. 4.71 + 1.2 = 5.91
8. 2.99 + 0.2 = 3.01
9. 17.41 + 6.3 = 23.71
10. 6.83 − 3.5 = 3.33
11. 4.7 − 2.61 = 2.09
12. 114.2 + 3.81 = 152.3
13. 17.2 − 6.8 = 10.4
14. 20.05 + 3.9 = 20.44

❓ Is That Correct?—Use estimation.

Round each number to the nearest one and mentally compute an answer. Put a checkmark next to all answers that are not close to the estimate.

Example: 4.2 − 3.9 ⟶ 4 − 4 = 0

The answer should be close to 0. Since 3 is not close to 0, this answer is wrong.

✓ Check Your Work—Use another strategy.

Rewrite each problem on a separate piece of paper. Write the problems vertically and align the decimals. Work the problems and compare your answers to Aleita's. Write the correct answer next to each problem she got wrong. For each of Aleita's wrong answers, find her mistake. Did she forget the decimal or put it in the wrong place? Did she forget to align the decimals before doing the arithmetic? Did she make a mistake borrowing or carrying?

Name _____ Date _____

<Number and Operations>

Adding and Subtracting Decimals

Error Alert! When adding or subtracting a whole number with a decimal, make sure the decimals are aligned. Any whole number can be written as a decimal.
   Example: 3 = 3.0
                29 = 29.0

Practice

Solve each addition and subtraction problem. (Hint: Write problems vertically and align the decimals.)

1. 14.5 + 7.21 = _____

2. 5 + 7.9 = _____

3. 10 − 8.2 = _____

4. 136.7 − 78.3 = _____

5. 17.4 + 50.09 = _____

6. 11.9 − 0.45 = _____

7. 9.32 + 14 = _____

8. 132 − 7.8 = _____

9. 36.6 + 4.89 = _____

10. 88.7 − 6.67 = _____

Check Your Work

Compare answers with a classmate. Correct any different answers. Be prepared to explain what kind of mistake was made.

Name _____ Date _____

(Number and Operations)

Multiplication

Problems: Find the products.

Cody's Answers:

1.   56
    × 4
    ─────
     224

2.   89
    × 2
    ─────
    1,618

2.   95
    × 3
    ─────
     275

2.   62
    × 2
    ─────
     124

2.   48
    × 4
    ─────
     192

2.   78
    × 3
    ─────
     243

? Is That Correct?—Use estimation.

Are Cody's answers reasonable? Round each 2-digit number to the tens place and use mental math. Put a star next to any answer that is not close to the estimated product.

Example: 56 × 4 ⟶ 60 × 4 = 240, which is close to 224

✓ Check Your Work—Use another strategy

Multiplication is repeated addition, which means adding the same number again and again. On another piece of paper, solve each problem using repeated addition. Then compare your answers to Cody's. Write the correct answer next to each problem he got wrong. Try to figure out what Cody did wrong.

Example: 56 × 4 = 56 + 56 + 56 + 56 = 224. Cody's answer was right.

© McGraw-Hill Children's Publishing

0-7424-2783-8 *Is That Correct?*

Multiplication

Problems: Find the products.

Tuyen's Answers:

1. 36
    × 5

    185

2. 87
    × 2

    164

3. 29
    × 6

    174

4. 61
    × 3

    183

5. 55
    × 8

    440

6. 17
    × 4

    64

7. 23
    × 9

    207

8. 45
    × 7

    283

Is That Correct?—Use estimation.

Are Tuyen's answers reasonable? Round each 2-digit number to the tens place and use mental math to multiply. Put a star next to any answer that is not close to the estimated product.

Example: 36 × 5 ⟶ 40 × 5 = 200, which is close to 185

Check Your Work—Use another strategy.

Cai decided to check Tuyen's answers by using a pull-apart strategy. She put the 2-digit numbers into its expanded form before multiplying.

Example: 36 = 30 + 6
  36 × 5 = 30 × 5 + 6 × 5
       =   150 + 30
       =   180

On another piece of paper, solve each of the problems using Cai's method. Then compare your answers to Tuyen's. Write the correct answer next to each problem she got wrong. Try to figure out what Tuyen did wrong.

Does estimation help you find all the mistakes? What kinds of mistakes does estimation help you find?

Name _____   Date _____

(NUMBER AND OPERATIONS)

Multiplication

ERROR ALERT! Carefully check each step. Did you perform each multiplication correctly? Did you add in each carried digit? Did you multiply by each number?

Example:
```
   2
  4 1 6
×     4
───────
  1,664
```

1) 4 × 6 = 24. Put down 4. Carry the 2.
2) 4 × 1 = 4 and 4 + 2 = 6. Put down 6.
3) 4 × 4 = 16. Put down 16.

PRACTICE

Find the products.

1. 416
  ×   4

2. 318
  ×   6

3. 379
  ×   2

4. 719
  ×   9

5. 168
  ×   7

6. 713
  ×   8

7. 219
  ×   6

8. 237
  ×   5

9. 245
  ×   3

Check Your Work

Use a different method to solve each problem. Compare the answers and decide which one is right.

Name _____ Date _____

<Number and Operations>

Multiplication

Error Alert! Carefully check each step. Did you perform each multiplication correctly? Did you add in each carried digit? Did you multiply by each number?

Example:
$$\begin{array}{r} \overset{1\,1}{4}23 \\ \times\ \ \ 6 \\ \hline 2{,}538 \end{array}$$

1) $3 \times 6 = 18$. Put down 8. Carry the 1.
2) $6 \times 2 = 12$ and $12 + 1 = 13$. Put down 3. Carry the 1.
3) $6 \times 4 = 24$ and $24 + 1 = 25$. Put down 25.

Practice

Find the products.

1. $\begin{array}{r} 423 \\ \times\ \ \ 6 \\ \hline \end{array}$

2. $\begin{array}{r} 735 \\ \times\ \ \ 3 \\ \hline \end{array}$

3. $\begin{array}{r} 817 \\ \times\ \ \ 9 \\ \hline \end{array}$

4. $\begin{array}{r} 325 \\ \times\ \ \ 5 \\ \hline \end{array}$

5. $\begin{array}{r} 316 \\ \times\ \ \ 8 \\ \hline \end{array}$

6. $\begin{array}{r} 326 \\ \times\ \ \ 6 \\ \hline \end{array}$

7. $\begin{array}{r} 623 \\ \times\ \ \ 4 \\ \hline \end{array}$

8. $\begin{array}{r} 231 \\ \times\ \ \ 7 \\ \hline \end{array}$

9. $\begin{array}{r} 687 \\ \times\ \ \ 3 \\ \hline \end{array}$

Check Your Work

Use a different method to solve each problem. Compare the answers and decide which one is right.

© McGraw-Hill Children's Publishing

0-7424-2783-8 *Is That Correct?*

Name _____ Date _____

(Number and Operations)

Division

Problem: Find the quotient using mental math.

Alejandro's Answer: 24 ÷ 6 = 3

✓ Check Your Work—Use a model.

Eduardo drew a model to check Alejandro's work. He drew 24 circles. Finish Eduardo's model by circling groups of 6.

○ ○ ○ ○ ○ ○ ○ ○ ○ ○ ○ ○
○ ○ ○ ○ ○ ○ ○ ○ ○ ○ ○ ○

1. How many groups of 6 can be made from 24 items? _____
   Was Alejandro's answer correct? _____

◉ Practice

Find the quotients using mental math.

2. 42 ÷ 7 = _____

3. 35 ÷ 5 = _____

4. 21 ÷ 3 = _____

5. 32 ÷ 8 = _____

6. 27 ÷ 9 = _____

✓ Check Your Work

Draw a model next to each problem. Compare each model to your answer. Which division facts do you need to study more?

© McGraw-Hill Children's Publishing   0-7424-2783-8 *Is That Correct?*

Name _____ Date _____

<Number and Operations>

Division

Problem: Use pencil and paper to find the quotient.

Alegria's Answer:

```
      3R9
   7)30
    -21
     ─────
      9
```

✓ Check Your Work—Use a model.

1. Check Alegria's answer by using the model. There are 30 squares shown here. Circle groups of 7. How many groups can you make? How many squares are left over?

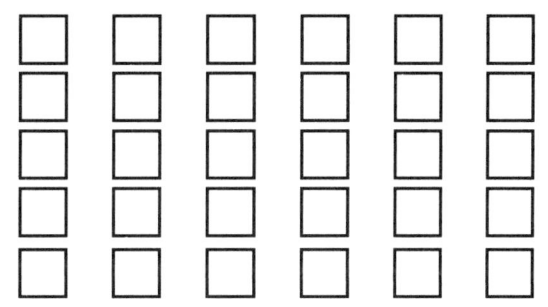

   □ □ □ □ □ □
   □ □ □ □ □ □
   □ □ □ □ □ □
   □ □ □ □ □ □
   □ □ □ □ □ □

2. Was Alegria's answer correct? _____

3. Check Alegria's arithmetic at each step. Did she make an arithmetic mistake? _____

   7 × 3 = _____

   30 − 21 = _____

4. Look at Alegria's remainder. Compare that to the divisor (7). What do you notice?

5. What mistake did Alegria make?

Error Alert! The remainder must be smaller than the divisor.

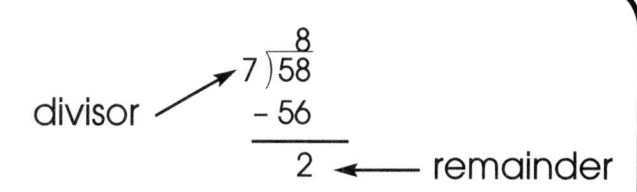

```
             8
          7)58
  divisor  -56
           ─────
            2  ← remainder
```

© McGraw-Hill Children's Publishing   0-7424-2783-8 *Is That Correct?*

Name _____ Date _____

(Number and Operations)

Division

Problem: Use mental math to find the quotient.

Adam's Answer: 66 ÷ 8 = 8 R2

Check Your Work—Work the problem backwards.

1. Check Adam's answer by working the problem backwards. Is Adam's answer correct? _____

   8 × 8 = _____ ____ + 2 = _____

Check Your Work—Use another method.

2. Use another method to check Adam's work. Describe the method you used.

Practice

Use mental math to find each quotient.

3. 74 ÷ 9 = _____   4. 55 ÷ 7 = _____   5. 39 ÷ 6 = _____

6. 21 ÷ 4 = _____   7. 15 ÷ 2 = _____   8. 47 ÷ 8 = _____

9. 20 ÷ 3 = _____   10. 59 ÷ 9 = _____ 11. 43 ÷ 7 = _____

12. 33 ÷ 6 = _____ 13. 30 ÷ 9 = _____ 14. 50 ÷ 8 = _____

Check Your Work

On another piece of paper, check each answer by working the problem backwards.

Name _____ Date _____

<Number and Operations>

Division

Practice

Find each quotient using mental math or pencil and paper.

1. 4)36

2. 7)49

3. 3)30

4. 8)72

5. 6)42

6. 2)14

7. 5)46

8. 9)35

9. 6)50

10. 8)44

11. 7)40

12. 4)22

Check Your Work

Check each answer using a method of your choice.

Name _____ Date _____

(Number and Operations)

Multiplication and Division

Practice

Find each product or quotient.

1. 92
   × 7
   ___

2. 8)̅7̅2̅

3. 76
   × 4
   ___

4. 512
   × 8
   ___

5. 3)̅3̅6̅

6. 415
   × 9
   ___

7. 7)̅4̅6̅

8. 883
   × 2
   ___

9. 6)̅2̅9̅

Check Your Work

List some strategies you could use to check the multiplication problems.
List some strategies you could use to check the division problems.
Check your answers using a strategy of your choice.

Name _____ Date _____

<Number and Operations>

Multiplication and Division

Practice

Find each product or quotient.

1. $\begin{array}{r} 84 \\ \times\ 3 \\ \hline \end{array}$

2. $6\overline{)36}$

3. $\begin{array}{r} 33 \\ \times\ 4 \\ \hline \end{array}$

4. $\begin{array}{r} 216 \\ \times\ \ \ 5 \\ \hline \end{array}$

5. $4\overline{)72}$

6. $\begin{array}{r} 861 \\ \times\ \ \ 7 \\ \hline \end{array}$

7. $8\overline{)36}$

8. $\begin{array}{r} 943 \\ \times\ \ \ 3 \\ \hline \end{array}$

9. $8\overline{)29}$

Check Your Work

List some strategies you could use to check the multiplication problems.
List some strategies you could use to check the division problems.
Check your answers using a strategy of your choice.

Name _____ Date _____

(Number and Operations)

Riddles

ERROR ALERT! Check the answer to make sure it meets every single condition.

Problem: I am a 4-digit number. I am less than 2,500 but greater than 1,200. The sum of my digits is 4. None of my digits are even. What number am I?

Miki's Answer: 2,011

Is That Correct?—Does the answer match the question?

1. Is Miki's answer a 4-digit number? _____

2. Is Miki's answer less than 2,500 but greater than 1,200? _____

3. Is the sum of the digits equal to 4? _____

4. Are none of the digits even? _____

5. Is Miki's answer correct? _____

6. Solve the problem correctly. _____

Practice

Solve the following riddles.

7. I am a 3-digit odd number between 710 and 720. My digits add up to 11. What number am I? _____

8. I am a 4-digit even number between 4,000 and 5,000. The sum of my digits is 20. The ones digit and the hundreds digit are the same. The tens digit and the thousands digit are the same. What number am I?

_____

Check Your Work

Compare answers with a classmate. Did you both get the same answer? Do your answers meet every condition?

© McGraw-Hill Children's Publishing

0-7424-2783-8 *Is That Correct?*

Name _____ Date _____

<Number and Operations>

Applications—Addition and Subtraction

Problem: Candelora's Mom owns a music store. Candelora helps her mom keep track of CDs at the store. There are 762 CD titles listed in the computer. Candelora enters 292 new titles. What is the total number of CD titles listed now?

Manuela's Answer: There are a total of 954 CD titles listed now.

```
  762
+ 292
-----
  954
```

Check Your Work—Use another strategy.

1. Did Manuela choose the correct math process (+, −, ×, ÷) to solve the problem? _____ What clue words in the problem tell you what process to use?

2. Use the pull-apart strategy to check Manuela's arithmetic. Did Manuela perform the process correctly?

   762 = 700 + _____ + _____

   + 292 = _____ + _____ + _____

   _____

   = _____ + _____ + _____ = _____

Practice

Solve each problem. Show your work. Trade papers with a classmate. Compare your answers.

3. One day, 278 CDs were sold. The next day, 183 CDs were sold. How many more CDs were sold on the first day?

4. The music store had 757 customers last month and 662 customers this month. How many customers did the store have all together in those two months?

© McGraw-Hill Children's Publishing   0-7424-2783-8 *Is That Correct?*

Name _____   Date _____

(NUMBER AND OPERATIONS)

Applications—Addition and Subtraction

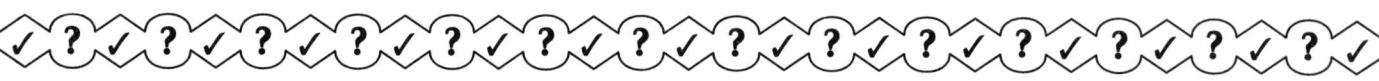

Problem: Raúl, Rico, and their dad are standing in line at the movie theater. There are 12 people in line. There are 4 people behind the family. How many people are in front of the family?

Carlos's Answer: There are 8 people in front of the family. 12 − 4 = 8

Is That Correct?—Put the answer back into the problem.

1. Put the answer back into the problem. There are 8 people in front of and 4 people in back of the 3 family members. This makes a total of _____ people.

2. Correct Carlos's answer. _____ What did Carlos forget when he solved the problem?

Practice

Solve each problem. Show your work. Write your answer in a complete sentence.

3. A child's ticket costs $3.75. An adult ticket costs twice that amount. How much did Raúl and Rico's dad pay for all their tickets?

4. A large popcorn costs $3.50. A medium soda costs $3.10. An Econo-combo contains a large popcorn and 2 medium sodas. It costs $9.50. How much money does the Econo-combo save?

Check Your Work

Check your answers. Prove your answers are correct by putting the answer back into the problem.

© McGraw-Hill Children's Publishing   0-7424-2783-8 *Is That Correct?*

Name _____ Date _____

<Number and Operations>

Applications—Multiplication

Problem: The students at Rockford Elementary are having a book sale. They are arranging the books into categories and stacking them on tables. Lina sorted books about sports. She had 8 stacks of 6 books each. How many sports books in all were at the sale?

Maya's Answer: There were 48 sports books in all. 8 × 6 = 48

Check Your Work—Use a model.

1. Did Maya use the correct process? _____ How do you know?

2. Draw a model of 8 stacks with 6 books each. Count all the books. Is Maya's arithmetic correct? _____

Practice

Solve each problem. Show your work.

3. Nina put the fiction books into 12 stacks of 10 books each. How many fiction books were at the sale?

4. Olivia had 12 stacks of picture books with 5 books in each stack. How many picture books were at the sale?

5. The book sale was in the gym. The students set up 9 rows of 4 tables each. How many tables were set up?

Check Your Work

Draw a model to prove that each of your answers is correct.

© McGraw-Hill Children's Publishing   0-7424-2783-8 *Is That Correct?*

Name _____ Date _____

(Number and Operations)

Applications—Division

Error Alert! If a story problem with division has a remainder, think about what the remainder means and then decide how it should affect the answer.

Problem: The 5 members of the Garcia family decided to visit Denali National Park for their summer vacation. All together, they will eat a total of 40 meals while they are at the park. How many meals will each person eat? If each person eats 3 meals a day, how many days will they stay at the park?

Jeremy's Answer: Each person will eat 8 meals. $40 ÷ 5 = 8$.
They will stay 2 days. $8 ÷ 3 = 2$ R2

Is That Correct?—Does the answer make sense?

1. Think about what each number in the process means. Write words with the numbers to make sure the answer makes sense. Does Jeremy's first answer make sense? _____

   40 meals ÷ 5 people = 8 meals per person

2. Look at Jeremy's second answer. Put the answer back in the problem to see if it makes sense. If they stay 2 days and each person eats 3 meals per day, how many meals per person is that? _____ Does this answer match your answer to question 1? _____

3. What did Jeremy forget to include in his answer?

Mark's Answer: The family will stay $2\frac{1}{2}$ days. They will leave after lunch on the third day.

4. Do you think Mark's answer is more accurate or less accurate than Jeremy's? _____ Why?

Name _____ Date _____

<Number and Operations>

Applications—Multiplication and Division

⊙ Practice

The 5 members of the Garcia family decided to visit Denali National Park for their summer vacation. Solve each problem. Show your work. Write each answer in a complete sentence.

1. Mr. Garcia bought a set of 24 postcards for everyone in the family to share. How many will each person get to send to friends back home? How many will be left to put in the family scrapbook?

2. The family went to a ranger talk. They learned that the park has 6 small herds with 17 moose in each herd. How many total moose live in the park?

3. There are 79 tourists going on the Horseshoe Lake walk. There are 8 rangers leading groups. Each ranger should have approximately the same number of tourists. How should they split up the tourists?

4. The family shared a sightseeing bus with other tourists. Each row on the bus had 4 seats. The bus was crowded. Eight of the rows were full. The ninth row had 3 of its seats filled. How many people were on the bus?

✓ Check Your Work

Draw a model to prove that each of your answers is correct.

Name _____ Date _____

(Algebra)

PATTERNS

Problem: Find the pattern. Write the next 3 numbers in the pattern. Write a rule for the pattern.

26   34   42   50

Yukios' Answer: 58, 67, 75   Rule: +8
Kiyoshi's Answer: 58, 66, 74   Rule: +8

Is That Correct?—Does the answer match the question?

1. Both students chose the same rule. Check to make sure the rule matches the pattern. Add 8 to each number. Do you get the next number in the pattern? _____

2. Kiyoshi chose different numbers in the pattern than Yukio. Which student made a mistake? _____ What did he do wrong?

3. Why is it important to check every number in your answer, even if you got the rule right?

Practice

Find the patterns. Write the next 3 numbers in each pattern. Write a rule for the pattern.

4. 99   198   297   396   ____   ____   ____   **Rule:** _____

5. 40   37   34   31   ____   ____   ____   **Rule:** _____

6. 115   100   85   70   ____   ____   ____   **Rule:** _____

Check Your Work

Check each answer carefully. Make sure the rule works between each pair of numbers, including the 3 new terms.

Name _____ Date _____

<Algebra>

PATTERNS

Problem: Find the pattern. Write the next 3 numbers in the pattern. Describe the pattern. 5, 9, 14, 23 . . .

Trevor's Answer: 27, 31, 35   **Rule:** Add 4 each time.

Is That Correct?—Does the answer match the question?

Trevor did very well on the patterns from page 52. He thinks he found a shortcut.

"Subtract the first two numbers to find the amount of change each time. If the pattern gets bigger, the rule is to add the change each time. If it gets smaller, the rule is to subtract that amount each time."

1. Do you think Trevor's method will work for all patterns? Why or why not?

2. Did Trevor's method work for this pattern? Check Trevor's rule. Does it work between each pair of numbers? _____

3. Should Trevor use his shortcut on all patterns? _____

4. Solve the problem correctly. Look for a different type of pattern.

Practice

Find the pattern. Write the next three numbers in the pattern. Use words to describe the pattern.

5. 7 9 12 16 21 _____ _____ _____   Rule: _____

Check Your Work

Compare answers with a classmate. Did you get the same answer? Did you describe the rules the same way?

Name _____ Date _____

(Algebra)

PATTERNS

Problem: Find the pattern. Write the next 3 numbers in the pattern. Write a rule for the pattern. 2, 4, 8, 16, 32

Lindsey's Answer: 64, 128, 256   Rule: × 2
Amy's Answer: 64, 128, 256   Rule: Add the same number again.

Is That Correct?—Does the answer match the question?

1. Compare Lindsey and Amy's answers.

2. Does either student have a correct answer? How do you know?

Amy's Answers: Amy found patterns for the following problems.

3. 4 12 36 <u>44</u> <u>52</u> <u>60</u>   Rule: + 8

4. 12,500 2,500 500 <u>100</u> <u>20</u> <u>4</u>   Rule: ÷ 5

5. 7 21 63 <u>189</u> <u>567</u> <u>1,701</u>   Rule: × 3

6. 5,120 1,280 320 <u>160</u> <u>80</u> <u>40</u>   Rule: ÷ 2

7. 3 6 12 <u>15</u> <u>18</u> <u>21</u>   Rule: + 3

8. 6 18 54 <u>162</u> <u>486</u> <u>1,458</u>   Rule: ÷ 3

Check Your Work

Check Amy's work. Put a checkmark next to each problem that is wrong. Then find the correct answer.

Name _____   Date _____

<Algebra>

COMMUTATIVE PROPERTY

ERROR ALERT! Commutative means to change the order. An operation is commutative only if you can change the order of the numbers and still get the same answer.
Example: 4 + 5 = 5 + 4 because 9 = 9.

Problems: Is each expression commutative? If it is, use the commutative property to rewrite the expression. If not, write "no."

Jack's Answers:

A. 3 + 5 = 5 + 3   B. 7 × 8 = 8 × 7   C. 5 − 3 = 3 − 5

D. 16 ÷ 4 = 24 ÷ 6   E. 7 + 2 = 2 + 7   F. 3 × 9 = 9 × 3

G. 4 − 1 = 1 − 4   H. 24 ÷ 4 = 4 ÷ 24   I. 3 + 2 = 4 + 1

Is That Correct?—Does the answer match the question?

Make sure Jack's answers are correct by checking to see that the answer is the same on both sides of the equal sign.

Example: 3 + 5 = 5 + 3
            8   =   8   The answers were the same.

1. Which problems have different answers?

Check each of Jack's answers to make sure he used the commutative property. The same numbers should be used, but in a different order.

Example: 16 ÷ 4 = 24 ÷ 6   Different numbers were used on both sides.

2. Which problems did not use the commutative property?

3. Correct Jack's mistakes. Remember to write "no" if changing the order of the numbers gives different answers. Which types of operations (+, −, ×, ÷) are commutative? _____

© McGraw-Hill Children's Publishing   0-7424-2783-8 *Is That Correct?*

Name _____ Date _____

(Algebra)

Associative Property

ERROR ALERT! Associative means to change the grouping. An operation is associative if changing the grouping doesn't change the answer. The order of the numbers stays the same, but the parentheses move.

Example: $(3 \times 2) \times 5 = 3 \times (2 \times 5)$
$6 \times 5 = 3 \times 10$
$30 = 30$

Problem: Is addition associative? Give an example to support your answer.

Jenna's Answer: Yes. Changing the order doesn't change the answer.

Does $(4 + 5) + 6 = (4 + 6) + 5$?
$9 + 6 = 10 + 5$
$15 = 15$ Yes.

Crystal's Answer: No. Changing the grouping does change the answer.

Does $(8 + 2) + 1 = 8 + (2 + 1)$?
$11 + 1 = 8 + 3$?
$12 \neq 11$ No.

? Is That Correct?—Know the correct definition.

1. Look at Jenna's answer. Did she use the correct definition for associative? Did the example she chose match the definition?

2. Look at Crystal's answer. Did she use the correct definition for associative? Did the example she chose match the definition?

3. Check Jenna's and Crystal's arithmetic. Is all of the addition correct?

Name _____ Date _____

<Algebra>

Associative Property

Practice

Answer the following questions. Give an example to support your answer.

1. Is addition associative?

2. Is subtraction associative?

3. Is multiplication associative?

Check Your Work

Check each of your answers against the following checklist.

- Did you use the correct definition of associative?
- Does your example match the definition?
    - Did you use one operation (+, −, or ×)?
    - Did you use three different numbers?
    - Did the numbers stay in the same order?
    - Did the parentheses change position?
- Did you perform the arithmetic correctly?

© McGraw-Hill Children's Publishing   0-7424-2783-8 *Is That Correct?*

Name _____ Date _____

(Algebra)

Function Tables

Problem: A function machine uses rules to change numbers. Look for a pattern in the IN and OUT numbers in each table. Fill in the table. Write the rule.

IN	78	15	41	22			55
OUT	65	2	28		24	3	

Brian's Answer:

IN	78	15	41	22	11	16	55
OUT	65	2	28	9	24	3	42

Rule: OUT = IN − 13

✓ Check Your Work—Look at the answer carefully.

1. Does Brian's rule work for all the number pairs given in the original problem? Test each pair to make sure.

    OUT = IN − 13: 65 = 78 − 13? _____

    2 = 15 − 13? _____

    28 = 41 − 13? _____

2. Check to make sure the numbers Brian put in the table are correct.

    OUT = IN − 13: 9 = 22 − 13? _____   ___ = ___ − 13? _____

    ___ = ___ − 13? _____   ___ = ___ − 13? _____

    ___ = ___ − 13? _____

3. Did Brian make any mistakes in his answer? If so, correct them.

Name _____ Date _____

<Algebra>

Function Tables

Practice

A function machine uses rules to change numbers. Look for a pattern in the IN and OUT numbers in each table. Fill in the table. Write the rule.

1.
IN	2	9	81	76	37		
OUT	11	18		85		34	51

Rule: _____

2.
IN	82	16	70	34	44		60
OUT	41	8			22	25	

Rule: _____

3.
IN	7	20	8		41		6
OUT		60	24	9		15	

Rule: _____

4.
IN	52		18		35		88
OUT	37	58	3	5		76	

Rule: _____

Check Your Work

Compare answers with a classmate's. Does the rule match each pair of given numbers? Do the numbers that were put into the table match the rule?

(Algebra)

Variables

Problems: Each problem has a letter in place of a number. Use what you know about addition, subtraction, multiplication, and division to find the missing number.

Hailey's Answers:

1. $3 + m = 29$
   $m = 32$

2. $33 + 17 = s - 8$
   $s = 58$

3. $55 - 18 = t$
   $t = 37$

4. $u \times 6 = 8 \times 3$
   $u = 58$

5. $b \div 20 = 4$
   $b = 80$

6. $75 - e = 30 + 5$
   $e = 35$

7. $24 \div c = 3 + 5$
   $c = 8$

8. $7 \times n = 2 \times 21$
   $n = 7$

9. $r - 48 = 12$
   $r = 60$

Is That Correct?—Put the answer back into the problem.

Check each of Hailey's answers. Put the answer back into the problem in place of the letter. Do the arithmetic. Check to make sure both sides are equal. Correct each problem Hailey got wrong.

Name _____ Date _____

<Algebra>

Variables

Practice

Each problem has a letter in place of a number. Use what you know about addition, subtraction, multiplication, and division to find the missing number.

1. $13 + m = 42$
   $m = $ _____

2. $41 + 28 = s - 7$
   $s = $ _____

3. $33 - 21 = t$
   $t = $ _____

4. $u \times 5 = 4 \times 10$
   $u = $ _____

5. $b \div 3 = 6$
   $b = $ _____

6. $88 - e = 21 + 8$
   $e = $ _____

7. $56 \div a = 8$
   $a = $ _____

8. $12 \times d = 30 + 6$
   $d = $ _____

9. $28 + 17 = 64 - g$
   $g = $ _____

10. $7 \times 4 = 2 \times j$
    $j = $ _____

Check Your Work

Check each of your answers. Put the answer into the problem in place of the letter. Do the arithmetic. Check to make sure both sides are equal. Correct each problem you got wrong.

© McGraw-Hill Children's Publishing   0-7424-2783-8 *Is That Correct?*

(Algebra)

Variables

Problem: Each of the symbols represents a number. Find the numbers that make both equations true.

🕷 × ❀ = 14 and 🕷 − ❀ = 5

Tremaine's Answer: 🕷 = 2 and ❀ = 7

Is That Correct?—Does the answer match the question?

1. Check Tremaine's answers by putting the answers back into both equations.

   🕷 × ❀ = 14   🕷 − ❀ = 5

   _____ × _____ = 14?   _____ − _____ = 5?

2. What mistake did Tremaine make? What should the correct answer be?

   🕷 = _____ and ❀ = _____.

Practice

Each of the symbols represents a number. Find the numbers that make both equations true.

3. ☼ × ★ = 48   ☼ = _____

   ☼ + ☼ = 12   ★ = _____

4. ▲ + ■ = 8   ▲ = _____

   ▲ ÷ ■ = 3   ■ = _____

Check Your Work

Check your work by putting your answers back into the equations.

Name _____ Date _____

<Algebra>

Variables

Practice

Each of the shapes represents a number. Find the numbers that make both equations true.

1. ▲ + ■ = 15
   ■ − ▲ = 1

   ▲ = _____
   ■ = _____

2. 3 × ⬓ = 15
   ▬ + ⬓ = 9

   ⬓ = _____
   ▬ = _____

3. ⬢ + ⬟ = 26
   ⬢ − ⬟ = 4

   ⬢ = _____
   ⬟ = _____

4. ● × ▰ = 32
   ● + ▰ = 12

   ● = _____
   ▰ = _____

5. 48 ÷ ⬣ = 8
   ⬣ × ◆ = 12

   ⬣ = _____
   ◆ = _____

Check Your Work

Check your work by putting your answers back into the equations.

Name _____ Date _____

(Algebra)

Applications—Writing Equations

Problem: A group of third-grade students got to vote for their favorite type of ice cream. Chocolate received twice as many votes as vanilla. Write an equation showing the relationship between the vanilla votes (V) and the chocolate votes (C).

Rakesha's Answer: $V = 2 \times C$

? Is That Correct?—Does the answer make sense?

Try putting numbers into the equation. Then look at the answer and see if it matches the problem.

1. Let's say there were 12 votes for chocolate. Put 12 in for C. How many votes were there for vanilla? _____

   $V = 2 \times \underline{} = \underline{}$

2. Now compare your answers to the problem. Did chocolate get twice as many votes as vanilla? _____

✓ Check Your Work—Test different answers.

3. Write the equation the way you think it should look.

4. If chocolate gets 12 votes, how many should vanilla get? _____

   Put your answers for chocolate and vanilla into your equation. Did you get a true equation? _____

5. If vanilla gets 10 votes, how many should chocolate get? _____
   Put your answers into your equation. Did you get a true equation? _____

Name _____ Date _____

<Algebra>

Applications—Writing Equations

PRACTICE

A group of third-grade students got to vote for their favorite type of ice cream. Write an equation that matches each situation. Use the variables given in the problem.

1. Some students voted for chocolate ice cream. The rest voted for strawberry. There were 24 votes all together.

   C = number of votes for chocolate   S = number of votes for strawberry

2. Orange sherbert ice cream received 5 more votes than lemon sherbert.

   O = number of votes for orange   L = number of votes for lemon

3. Butter pecan ice cream received 7 fewer votes than mint chocolate-chip ice cream.

   B = number of votes for butter pecan   M = number of votes for mint chocolate-chip

4. Rocky road ice cream received 3 times as many votes as toffee.

   R = number of votes for rocky road   T = number of votes for toffee

Check Your Work

Check to make sure each equation fits the situation. For each problem, find two numbers that fit the situation. Put the numbers into your equation. Does the equation work? Then try a second pair of numbers.

Name _____ Date _____

(Algebra)

Applications—Writing Equations

Problem: Jaleesa and her mom biked to the ice cream shop. Then they biked to the mall. They biked 18 miles all together.

A. It is s miles to the ice cream shop. It is m miles from the ice cream shop to the mall. Write an equation showing the relationship.

B. If it was 7 miles from the ice cream shop to the mall, how far was it to the ice cream shop? Write an equation. Then find the answer.

Dante's Answers: **A.** $s + m = 18$ **B.** $s + 7 = 18$; $s = 11$

❓ Is That Correct?—Does the answer make sense?

1. Look at Dante's answer to part **A**. Think about what each letter in the equation means. Read the equation out loud. Does the equation match the situation? _____

$$s + m = 18$$

? miles to the ice cream shop + ? miles to the mall = a total of 18 miles

2. Look at Dante's answer to part **B**. Think about what the letter and numbers in the equation mean. Read the equation out loud. Does the equation match the situation? _____

$$s + 7 = 18$$

? _____ + 7 = a total of 18 miles

✓ Check Your Work—Put the answer back into the problem.

3. Look at the second part of Dante's answer to part **B**. Put his answer back into the equation. Is the equation true? _____

$$s + 7 = 18$$

____ + 7 = 18?

© McGraw-Hill Children's Publishing

Applications—Writing Equations

<Algebra>

Practice

1. Shanequa and Martel like to collect basketball cards. Shanequa has 12 more cards than Martel.

   A. Shanequa has *s* cards and Martel has *m* cards. Write an equation showing this relationship.

   B. If Shanequa has 45 cards, how many cards does Martel have? Write an equation. Then find the answer.

2. Kaven likes to eat popsicles. He ate 5 more popsicles on Thursday than he ate on Wednesday.

   A. Kaven ate *w* popsicles on Wednesday and *t* popsicles on Thursday. Write an equation showing this relationship.

   B. If Kaven ate 8 popsicles on Thursday, how many popsicles did he eat on Wednesday? Write an equation. Then find the answer.

3. Atoya and Chantelle are both excellent soccer players. Combined, they scored 9 goals in one season.

   A. Atoya scored *a* goals and Chantelle scored *c* goals. Write an equation showing the relationship.

   B. If Atoya scored 5 goals, how many goals did Chantelle score? Write an equation. Then find the answer.

Check Your Work

Check your answers. Does each equation match the situation? Is the equation true when you put the answer back in?

(Algebra)

Applications—Graphing

Problem: Jordan is saving up money to buy a new portable CD player. Study the information in the table and make a line graph of the data. Then answer the question.

Week	1	2	3	4	5
Amt. Saved	$5	$13	$19	$24	$30

Between which two-week period did Jordan save the most? The least?

Luke's Answer: Jordan saved the same amount each week.

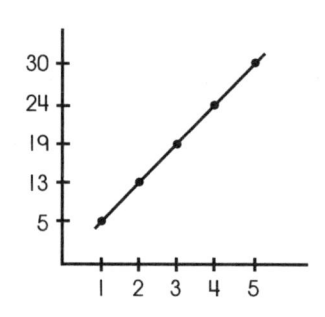

Is That Correct?—Does the answer make sense?

1. Compare Luke's answer to his graph. Does his answer appear to match the graph he drew? _____

2. Now look at the table. Find out how much he saved from one week to the next.

3. Does Luke's answer match the table? What should the answer be?

4. What is wrong with Luke's graph?

Error Alert! Make sure the numbers on the graph go up by the same amount each time.

Name _____   Date _____

<Algebra>

Applications—Graphing

PRACTICE

Anjelica borrowed $30 from her mother to buy a video game. She pays back some of the money each week from her allowance. Study the information in the table and make a line graph of the data. Then answer the questions.

Week	Amount Owed
0	$30
1	$28
2	$25
3	$18
4	$15
5	$10
6	$4
7	$0

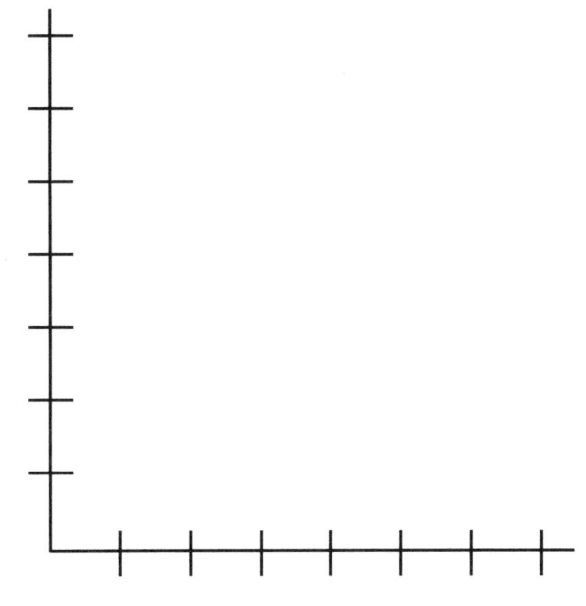

1. Did Anjelica pay back the same amount each week or did she pay back different amounts?

2. Between which two weeks did Anjelica pay the most? The least? Check your answers against the following checklist.

Check Your Work

- Did you label your graph with Weeks and Amount Owed?
- Did you include a correct scale?
    - Do the numbers go high enough?
    - Do the numbers go up by the same amount each time?
- Did you plot each point in the right place?
- Do your answers match both the graph and the table?

Name _____ Date _____

(Geometry)

Similar and Congruent

Error Alert! Similar figures are the same shape, but different sizes. Congruent figures are the same shape and the same size.

Problems: Classify each pair below as congruent, similar, or neither.

A. 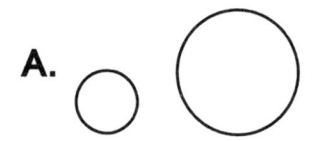 B.  C.

Luis's Answers:

A. congruent   B. similar   C. neither

Check Your Work—Use another strategy.

1. Check your answers. Use a piece of tracing paper. Trace one figure. Put the trace copy over the other figure. If they match up exactly, then they are congruent. Which of Luis's answers are incorrect? Correct any answers he got wrong.

Practice

Classify each pair below as congruent, similar, or neither.

2. 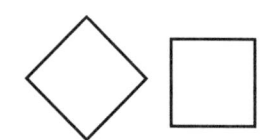   3.    4.

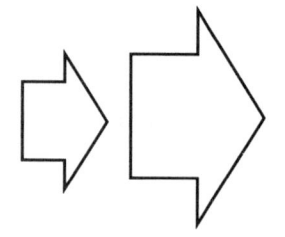

_____   _____   _____

Check Your Work

Compare answers with a classmate. Work out any differences.

Name _____ Date _____

<Geometry>

Similar and Congruent

Practice

Classify each pair below as congruent, similar, or neither.

1.

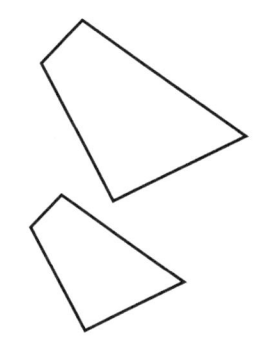

2.

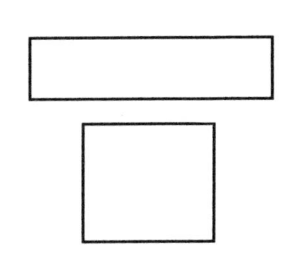

3.

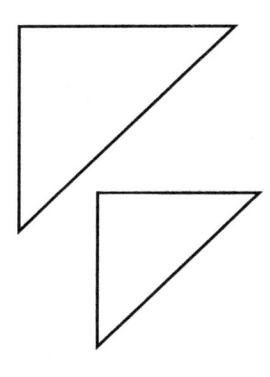

_____ _____ _____

4.

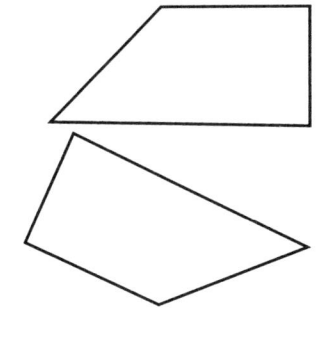

5.

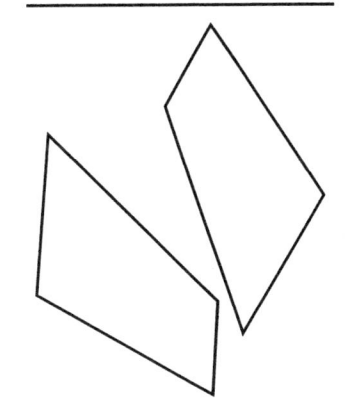

6.

_____ _____ _____

7.

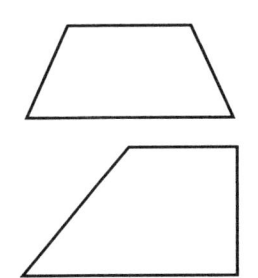

8.

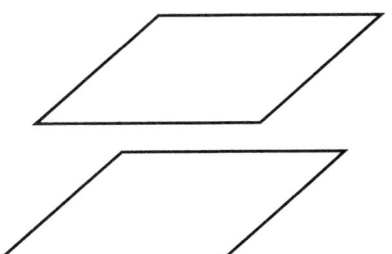

9.

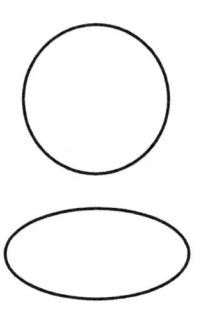

_____ _____ _____

Check Your Work

Use tracing paper to check your answers.

© McGraw-Hill Children's Publishing

0-7424-2783-8 *Is That Correct?*

Name _____ Date _____

(GEOMETRY)

SYMMETRY

Problem: How many lines of symmetry does the star have? Draw all dotted lines of symmetry on the shape.

Amari's Answer: There are 3 lines of symmetry.

Check Your Work—Use another strategy.

Trace a copy of Amari's star onto a small square of tracing paper.

1. Fold along each line of symmetry and check to make sure the two halves match up. Are the lines Amari drew actual lines of symmetry?

2. Try folding the star in other ways. Can you find any more lines of symmetry?

3. How many lines of symmetry does the star have? _____

Practice

How many lines of symmetry does each shape have? Draw all dotted lines of symmetry on each shape. Use tracing paper to check your answers.

4.   5.   6.

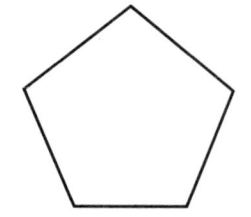

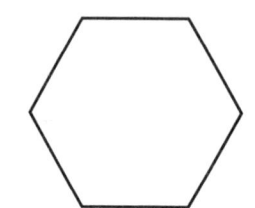

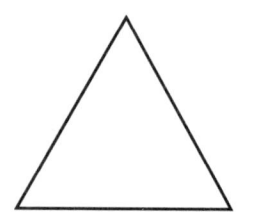

_____   _____   _____

© McGraw-Hill Children's Publishing   0-7424-2783-8 *Is That Correct?*

Name _____ Date _____

<Geometry>

SYMMETRY

Problems: Draw a dotted line of symmetry on each shape.

Amish's Answers:

1. 
2. 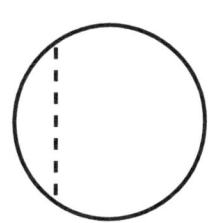
3. 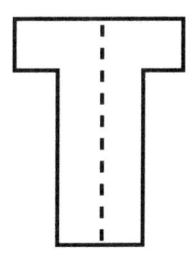
4. 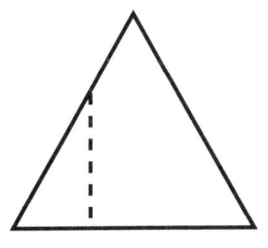
5. 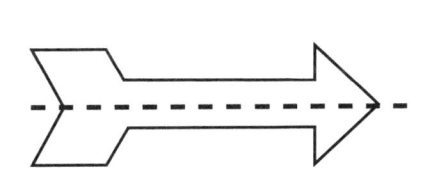
6. 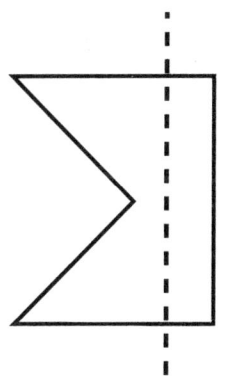
7. 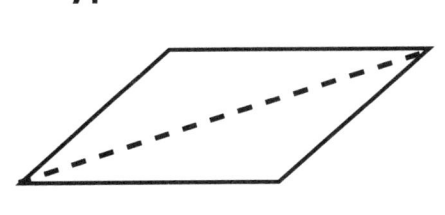
8. 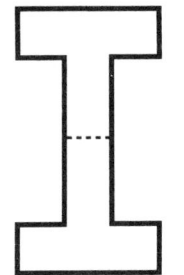
9.

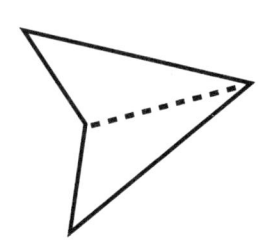

✓ Check Your Work—Use another strategy.

Trace each shape and the dotted line on a piece of tracing paper. Fold along each dotted line and check to make sure the two halves match up. Put a checkmark next to each wrong answer. For each of these problems, draw in a correct line of symmetry.

© McGraw-Hill Children's Publishing

0-7424-2783-8 *Is That Correct?*

Name _____ Date _____

(GEOMETRY)

Reflections and Rotations

ERROR ALERT! In a reflection, the figure is flipped over. In a rotation, the figure is turned.

Problems: For the drawings below, write reflection or rotation to describe how the figure was moved.

Beth's Answers:

A. reflection: E Ǝ

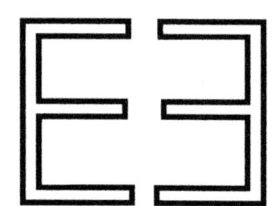

B. reflection: 5 ऽ

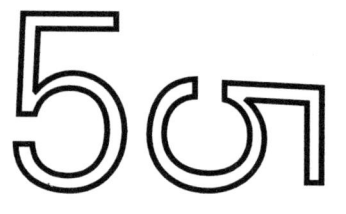

✓ Check Your Work—Use another strategy

Check Beth's answers.

1. Check to see if the image is a reflection. Trace the first shape on a piece of tracing paper. Try flipping the tracing paper onto the second image. If it matches, then it is a reflection. Which drawing shows a reflection? _____

2. Check to see if the image is a rotation. Trace the first shape on a piece of tracing paper. Try turning the tracing paper so it matches the second image. If it matches, then it is a rotation. Which drawing shows a rotation? _____

© McGraw-Hill Children's Publishing

0-7424-2783-8 Is That Correct?

Name _____   Date _____

<Geometry>

Reflections and Rotations

Practice

Look at each drawing below. Write reflection or rotation to describe how the figure was moved.

1.

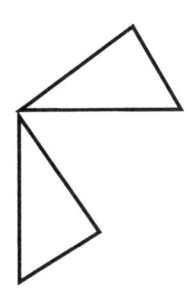

2.

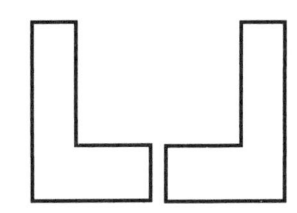

3.

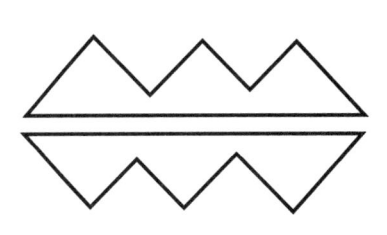

_____   _____   _____

4.

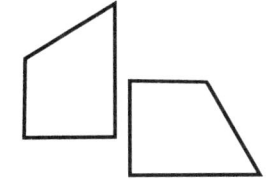

5.

6.

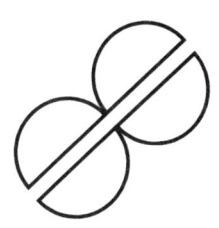

_____   _____   _____

Check Your Work

Use tracing paper to check your answers.

© McGraw-Hill Children's Publishing   0-7424-2783-8 *Is That Correct?*

Name _____   Date _____

(GEOMETRY)

Types of Triangles

Problems: Classify each type of triangle as isosceles, scalene, or equilateral based on its side lengths.

Dan's Answers:

A.

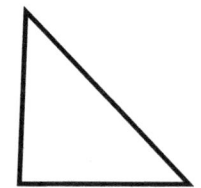

B.

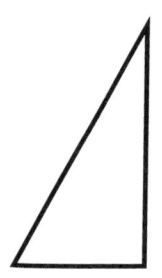

C.

equilateral   scalene   equilateral

❓ Is That Correct?—Know the correct definitions.

Look up the definition for each triangle type.

1. An equilateral triangle has _____ equal sides.

2. An isosceles triangle has _____ equal sides.

3. A scalene triangle has _____ equal sides.

4. Do you think all Dan's answers are correct? Correct any mistakes he might have made.

✓ Check Your Work—Take accurate measurements.

Use a ruler and measure all three sides of each triangle. Then check Dan's answers. Correct any of his mistakes. Did you find any mistakes with the ruler that you missed by just looking at the shapes?

Name _____ Date _____

<Geometry>

Types of Triangles

Practice

Look at each triangle. Classify each type of triangle as isosceles, scalene, or equilateral based on its side lengths.

1.

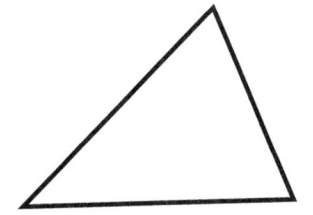

2.

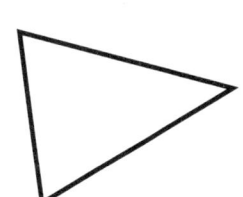

3.

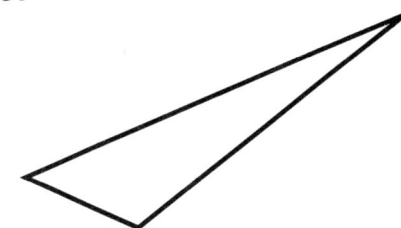

_____   _____   _____

4.

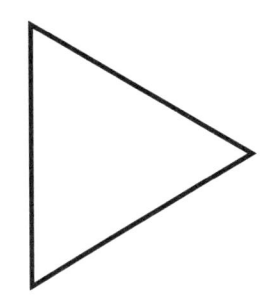

5.

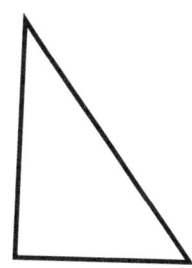

6.

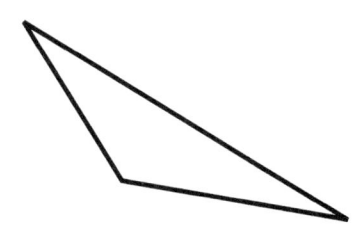

_____   _____   _____

Check Your Work

Measure the sides of each triangle to the nearest tenth of a centimeter. Then check your answers

Name _____ Date _____

(GEOMETRY)

Polygons

Problems: A polygon is a flat 2-dimensional figure made up of 3 or more line segments. The sides of a polygon are connected end-to-end and make a closed path. The sides of a polygon do not cross. Which of the following shapes are polygons?

Luisa's Answers:

A.

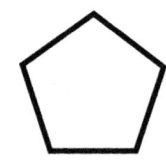

not a polygon

B.

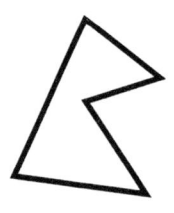

polygon

C.

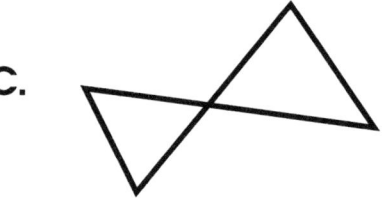

polygon

Is That Correct?—Does the answer match the question?

1. Read the definition for a polygon again. Then look at Luisa's answers. Do you think her answers are all correct? _____ Why or why not?

Look at each shape carefully. In order to be a polygon, the shape must match every characteristic in the definition.

2. Answer each of these questions for shapes **A, B,** and **C**.

   Is it made up of 3 or more   A. ____ B. ____ C. ____
   line segments (no curves)?

   Is it closed (no open edges)?   A. ____ B. ____ C. ____

   Are the sides NOT crossed?   A. ____ B. ____ C. ____

3. Which shapes are polygons? _____

Name _____   Date _____

<Geometry>

Polygons

Practice

For each shape, write polygon or not a polygon.

1. _____

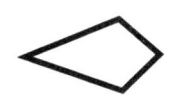

2. _____

3. _____

4. _____

5. _____

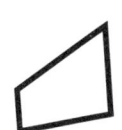

6. _____

7. _____

8. _____

9. _____

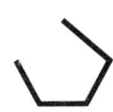

Check Your Work

Check each shape against the following checklist. The shape must match each characteristic in order to be a polygon.

- Is it made up of 3 or more line segments (no curves)?
- Is it closed (no open edges)?
- Are the sides NOT crossed?

For each shape that is not a polygon, be prepared to explain which characteristic it fails.

Name _____ Date _____

(GEOMETRY)

3-Dimensional Shapes

ERROR ALERT! Make sure you know your terminology. A face is any flat surface on a 3-dimensional shape. An edge is a line segment or curve where two faces meet. A vertex is a corner of the shape.

Problem: Use the clues. Write the name of the 3-dimensional shape.
I can roll.
I have 2 circular faces.
I can be stacked on top of a cube.
What shape am I?

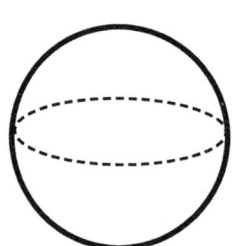

Jong-Min's Answer: A sphere

Is That Correct?—Does the answer match the question?

Compare the sphere to each of the clues. Make sure all the clues describe the sphere.

1. Can a sphere roll? _____

2. Does a sphere have 2 circular faces (flat surfaces shaped like circles)? _____

3. Could a sphere be stacked on a cube without falling off? _____

4. Is Jong-Min's answer correct? _____

5. Look at the shapes below. Choose the shape that best fits the clues given in the problem. Make sure the shape you choose matches every clue.

A. hemisphere

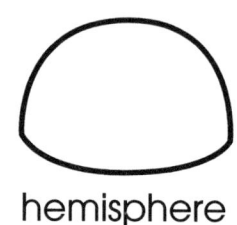

B. cylinder

C. cone

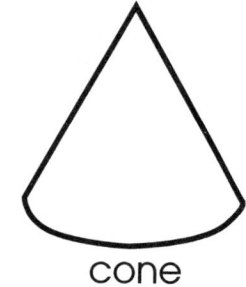

© McGraw-Hill Children's Publishing

0-7424-2783-8 Is That Correct?

Name _____   Date _____

<Geometry>

3-Dimensional Shapes

Error Alert! Make sure you know your terminology. A face is any flat surface on a 3-dimensional shape. An edge is a line segment where two faces meet. A vertex is a corner of the shape.

Use the clues and the pictures. Below each problem, write the name of the mystery shape that matches the clues.

1. I have 6 rectangle faces.
   I have 2 hexagon faces.
   I can be stacked on top of a cube.

   _____

2. I have 4 triangle faces.
   I have 1 rectangle face.
   I can't roll.

   _____

3. I have 6 rectangle faces.
   I am not a cube.
   I have 2 more vertices than faces.

   _____

4. I have 3 rectangle faces.
   I have 2 triangle faces.
   I can be stacked.

   _____

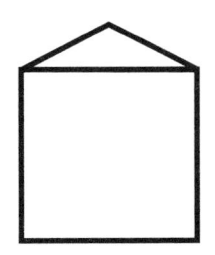

triangular prism 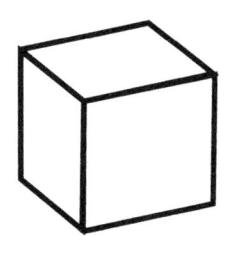   **cube** 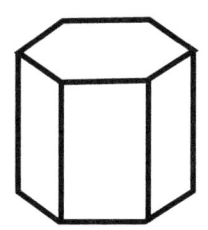   **hexagonal prism**

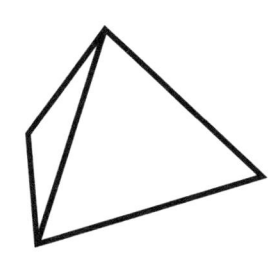

triangular pyramid 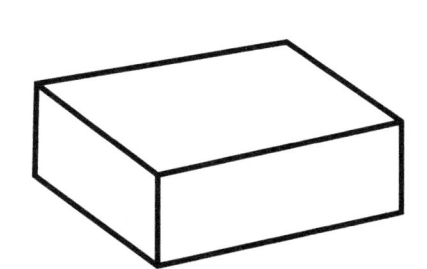   **rectangular prism** 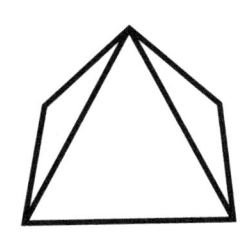   **rectangular pyramid**

© McGraw-Hill Children's Publishing   0-7424-2783-8 *Is That Correct?*

Name _____   Date _____

(GEOMETRY)

Applications—Point of View

Problem: This is a model of a new building. Draw the top, front, and right side views of the building.

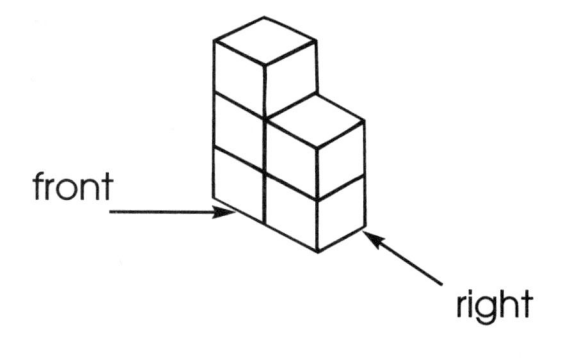

Anika's Answer:

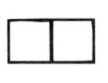

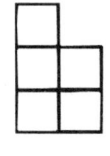

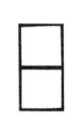

top   front   right side

✓ Check Your Work—Use a model.

Use cubes to build a model of the building. Face the front of the building towards you. Answer the questions and then make any needed corrections to Anika's drawing.

1. Put the model at eye-level and look directly at it from the front. Does Anika's front view match what you see? _____

2. Look down on the building from above. Does Anika's top view match what you see? _____

3. Put the model at eye-level and look directly at its right side. Does Anika's right side view match what you see? _____

⊙ Practice

4. Use the grid to draw the top, front, and right side views of the building. Then build a model to check your answer.

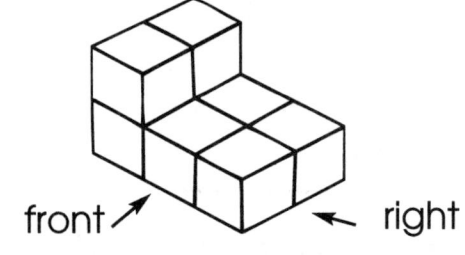

Name _____   Date _____

<Geometry>

Applications—Nets

Problem: Which cube could be created from this net?

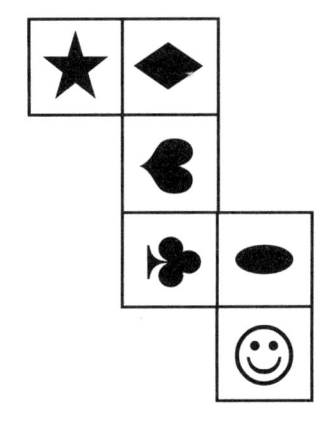

A.    B.    C.

Ke-Andre's Answer: B

Check Your Work—Use a model.

Make a copy of the net. Cut it out and fold it into a cube. Use transparent tape to tape the sides together.

1. Check Ke-Andre's answer. Position the cube so that the star is on the top, as shown on cube **B**. Can you twist the cube to show the clover and diamond as they appear on cube **B**? _____

2. Check to see if the cube can be positioned to look like cube **A** or cube **C**. Can your cube be positioned to look like either of these views? _____

Practice

3. Which cube can be created from this net?

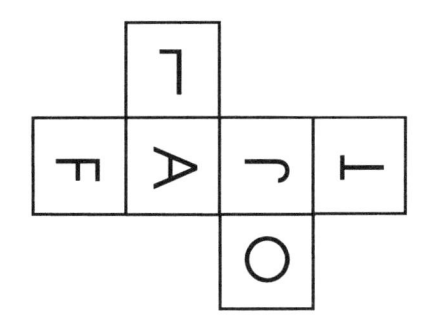

A.    B.    C.

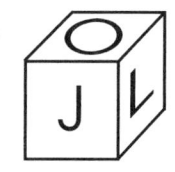

© McGraw-Hill Children's Publishing   0-7424-2783-8 *Is That Correct?*

Name _____   Date _____

<Geometry>

Applications—Using a Grid

Problem: The letters **M**, **N**, and **O** represent the houses of three friends—Matt, Nate, and Owen. Each square on the grid represents a square mile. The heavy black lines represent roads. Traveling the shortest distance along the roads, what is the distance in miles from Matt's house to Nate's house?

Chad's Answer: 15 miles
Todd's Answer: 7 miles
Jeff's Answer: 4 miles

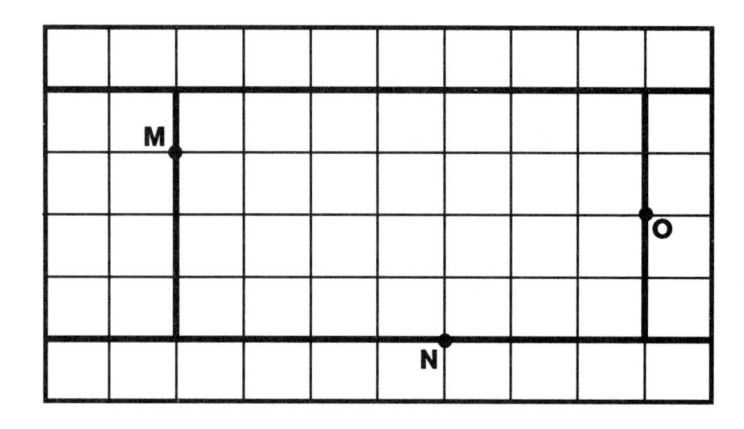

Is That Correct?—Does the answer match the question?

1. See if you can find the path each student used. Check to see if each answer matches the question.

	Chad	Todd	Jeff
Did he travel along the roads?	_____	_____	_____
Is his distance accurate?	_____	_____	_____
Is it the shortest distance?	_____	_____	_____

2. Which student had the correct answer? _____

© McGraw-Hill Children's Publishing   0-7424-2783-8 *Is That Correct?*

Name _____ Date _____

<Geometry>

Applications—Using a Grid

Practice

The letters **M**, **N**, and **O** represent the houses of three friends—Matt, Nate, and Owen. Each square on the grid represents a square mile. The heavy black lines represent roads. Use the grid to help you answer the questions.

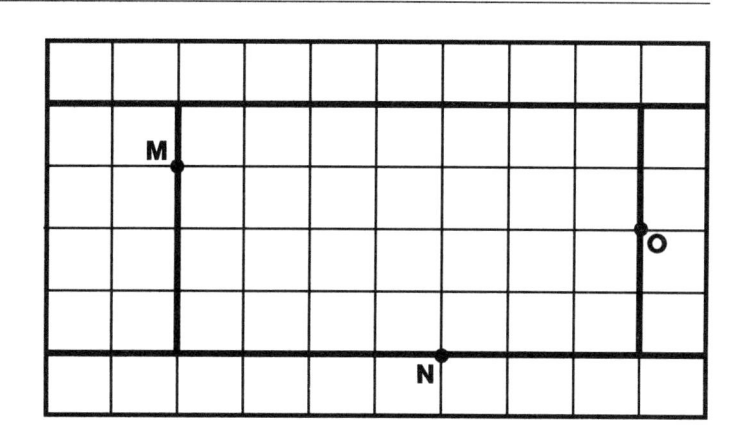

1. Traveling the shortest distance along the roads, what is the distance in miles between Owen's house and Nate's house? _____

2. Traveling the shortest distance along the roads, what is the distance in miles from Matt's house to Owen's house? _____

3. Traveling the longest distance along the roads, without tracing any part of the trip, what is the distance in miles between Owen's house and Nate's house? _____

4. Traveling the longest distance along the roads, without tracing any part of the trip, what is the distance in miles between Matt's house and Nate's house? _____

Check Your Work

Make sure your answers match each part of the question.

Name _____ Date _____

(GEOMETRY)

Applications—Coordinate Graphing

Problem: The map shows the location of some town landmarks. Give the coordinates of each landmark.

Latisha's Answers:

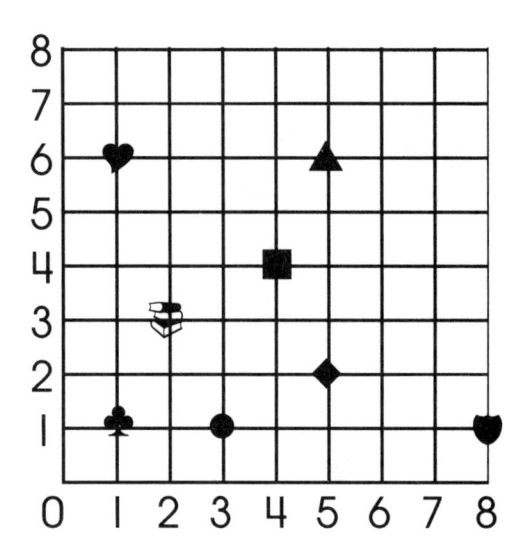

1. ♥ = school: (1, 6)
2. ▲ = museum: (6, 5)
3. ♣ = statue: (1, 1)
4. ● = lake: (3, 1)
5. ♦ = house: (2, 5)
6. ■ = store: (5, 3)
7. 📚 = library: (2, 3)
8. ♘ = gas station (8, 2)

Error Alert! In a coordinate pair (x, y), the first number (x) tells you how far to move to the right of 0. The second number (y) tells you how far to move up.

Check Your Work—Look the answer over carefully.

Check each of Latisha's answers. Put your finger on (0, 0). Look at Latisha's first number. Move your finger to the right that many spaces. Look at Latisha's second number. Move your finger up that many spaces. Check to make sure you land on the symbol that matches the landmark. Correct any of Latisha's wrong answers.

Name _____ Date _____

<Geometry>

Applications—Coordinate Graphing

Practice

The students in room 14 are going on a scavenger hunt at Willow Lake. Each team needs to find the objects below. Give the coordinates where each object can be found.

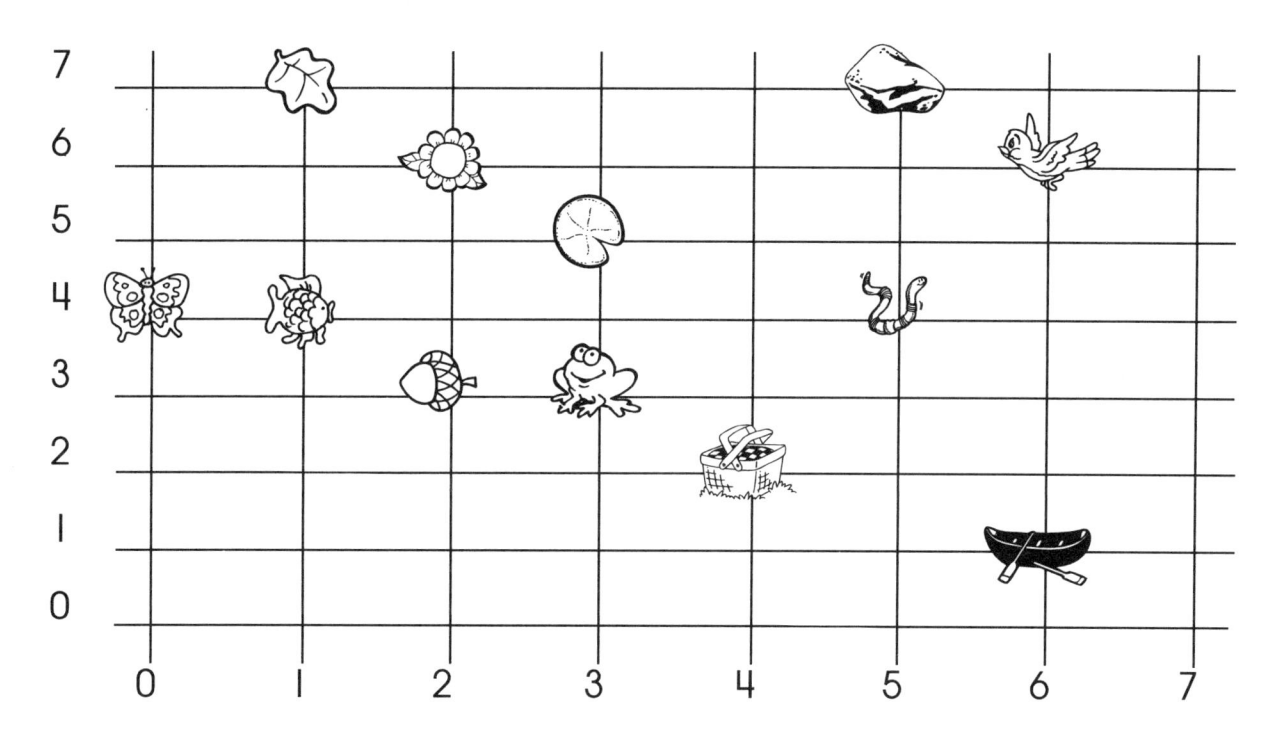

1. acorn _____
2. frog _____
3. worm _____
4. lily pad _____
5. boat _____
6. picnic basket _____

7. rock _____
8. butterfly _____
9. flower _____
10. leaf _____
11. fish _____
12. bird _____

Check Your Work

Compare answers with a classmate. If there are any differences, check your work and decide on a correct answer.

Name _____   Date _____

(MEASUREMENT)

AREA AND PERIMETER

Problem: Is the following statement true or false? Explain your reasoning. Give evidence to support your answer. *If two rectangles have the same perimeter, then they also have the same area.*

Rosa's Answer: The statement is true. Two rectangles with the same perimeter are really the same rectangle. So, they will have the same area.

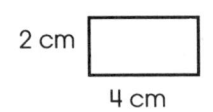

2 cm [rectangle] 4 cm

4 cm [rectangle] 2 cm

P = 2 + 4 + 2 + 4 = 12 cm
A = 4 × 2 = 8 sq cm²

P = 4 + 2 + 4 + 2 = 12 cm
A = 4 × 2 = 8 sq cm²

Is That Correct?—Is there enough proof?

1. Look at Rosa's example. Did she perform the calculations correctly? Does her example support her answer?

2. Do you think Rosa's example is enough to prove that the statement is true? Why or why not?

Nina's Answer: The statement is false. Both have a perimeter of 12 cm. But, one has an area of 8 sq cm, and one has an area of 9 sq cm.

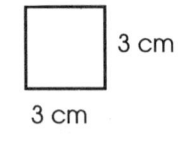

2 cm [rectangle] 4 cm

3 cm [square] 3 cm

P = 2 + 4 + 2 + 4 = 12 cm
A = 4 × 2 = 8 sq cm

P = 3 + 3 + 3 + 3 = 12 cm
A = 3 × 3 = 9 sq cm

3. Look at Nina's example. Did she perform the calculations correctly? Does her example support her answer? _____

4. You decide. Which student's answer is incorrect, and why?

Name _____ Date _____

<MEASUREMENT>

Area and Perimeter

Practice

Are the following statements true or false? Explain your reasoning. Give evidence to support your answer.

1. If each side of a rectangle is doubled, the perimeter is also doubled.

2. If each side of a rectangle is doubled, the area is also doubled.

3. If two rectangles have the same area, then they also have the same perimeter.

Error Alert! To prove a statement false, you only have to show one case that does not work. To prove a statement true, you need to give some reasoning about why it is true in every case.

© McGraw-Hill Children's Publishing

0-7424-2783-8 *Is That Correct?*

Name _____ Date _____

(MEASUREMENT)

VOLUME

Problem: Find the volume of the box. Show your work.

Antwan's Answer: The volume is 72 cubic feet since 4 × 6 × 3 = 72.

3 ft.
4 ft.
6 ft.

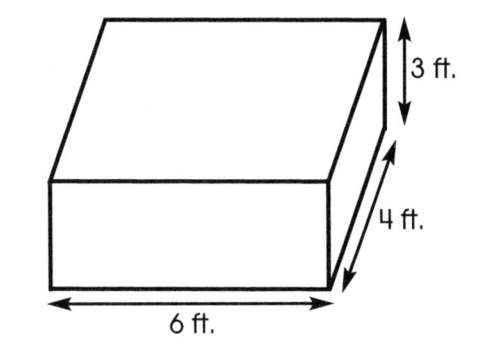

✓ Check Your Work—Use a model.

Use cubes to build a scale model to match the diagram. In the model, let each cube represent 1 cubic foot. Build one layer at a time.

1. How many cubes are in the bottom layer? _____

2. How many layers of cubes will there be? _____

3. How many total cubes are in the structure? _____

4. Did Antwan get the right answer? _____

⊙ Practice

Find the volume of the box. Show your work.

5.
4 ft.
2 ft.
4 ft.

✓ Check Your Work

Use cubes to build a scale model to match the diagram. Use the model to check your answer.

© McGraw-Hill Children's Publishing

0-7424-2783-8 *Is That Correct?*

Name _____ Date _____

<MEASUREMENT>

VOLUME

PRACTICE

Find the volume of each box. Show your work.

1. 8 in. × 5 in. × 3 in.

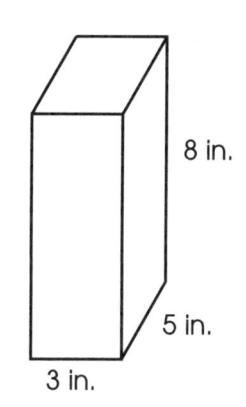

2. 8 in. × 4 in. × 3 in.

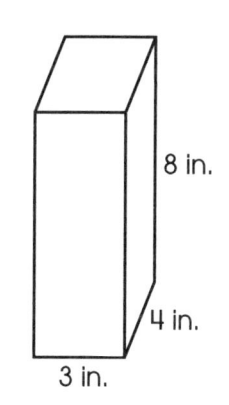

3. 6 in. × 4 in. × 4 in.

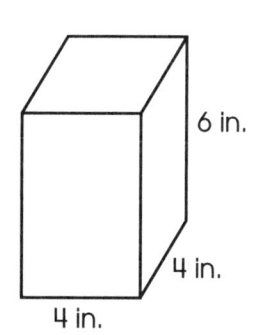

4. 4 in. × 2 in. × 7 in.

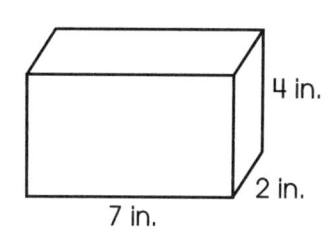

5. 6 in. × 1 in. × 7 in.

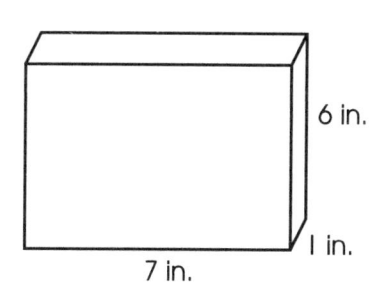

6. 4 in. × 2 in. × 8 in.

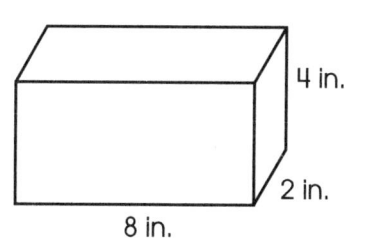

Check Your Work

Use cubes to build a scale model to match the diagram. Use the model to check your answer.

© McGraw-Hill Children's Publishing   0-7424-2783-8 *Is That Correct?*

Name _____ Date _____

(MEASUREMENT)

CUSTOMARY UNITS

ERROR ALERT! Capacity measures how much space a liquid takes up. It is measured in cups, pints, quarts, and gallons. Length is a measure of distance. It is measured in inches, feet, yards, and miles. Weight measures how heavy an object is. It is measured in ounces, pounds or tons.

Problem: What kind of unit best measures the amount of milk in this container?

Taylor's Answer: pounds
Hannah's Answer: cups
Brittany's Answer: gallons

Is That Correct?—Does the answer make sense?

Make sure the answer matches the type of measurement: length, capacity, or weight.

1. What type of measurement does the problem require? _____

2. Which student's answer is not the correct type of measurement?
_____

Make sure the answer matches the size of the object being measured. Compare Hannah's and Brittany's answers.

3. Which is smaller, cups or gallons? _____

4. Look at the picture of the milk container. Imagine what the real container looks like. Which unit is better for measuring the size of this container, cups or gallons? _____

© McGraw-Hill Children's Publishing

0-7424-2783-8 *Is That Correct?*

Name _____ Date _____

<MEASUREMENT>

CUSTOMARY UNITS

ERROR ALERT! Capacity measures how much space a liquid takes up. It is measured in cups, pints, quarts, and gallons. Length is a measure of distance. It is measured in inches, feet, yards, and miles. Weight measures how heavy an object is. It is measured in ounces, pounds or tons.

PRACTICE

Choose the units that would best measure each object. Not all units will be used.

_____ 1. weight of a bag of apples

_____ 2. short distance race

_____ 3. liquid baby medicine

_____ 4. weight carried by a semi-truck

_____ 5. punch in a punch bowl

_____ 6. single serving of chocolate milk

_____ 7. distance between two cities

_____ 8. diameter of a CD

_____ 9. melted butter used in a batch of cookies

_____ 10. height of a doorway

A. inches
B. cups
C. pounds
D. gallon
E. feet
F. miles
G. pints
H. tablespoons
I. tons
J. yards
K. quarts
L. ounces
M. teaspoons

Look at each of your answers carefully. Did you choose the right type of measurement for each object? Did you choose the correct unit size for each object?

Name _____ Date _____

(MEASUREMENT)

METRIC UNITS

ERROR ALERT! The base units of measurement are meters (length), liters (capacity), and grams (mass). The prefixes *milli* and *kilo* in front of a base unit help determine size.

milli = 1,000 times smaller than the base

kilo = 1,000 times larger than the base

Problem: What kind of unit best measures how much a computer weighs?

Alfonso's Answer: liters
Estefan's Answer: grams
Matteo's Answer: kilometers
Felipe's Answer: kilograms

Is That Correct?—Does the answer make sense?

Make sure the answer matches the type of measurement: length, capacity, or mass.

1. What type of measurement does the problem require? _____

2. Which students did not choose the correct type of measurement?
   _____

Make sure the answer matches the size of the object being measured. Compare Estefan's and Felipe's answers.

3. Which is smaller, grams or kilograms? _____

4. A fishing weight is about 1 gram. A kilogram weighs 1,000 times more than a gram. Which unit is better for measuring the weight of a computer, grams or kilograms? _____

94

© McGraw-Hill Children's Publishing

0-7424-2783-8 *Is That Correct?*

Name _____ Date _____

<MEASUREMENT>

METRIC UNITS

ERROR ALERT! The base units of measurement are meters (length), liters (capacity), and grams (mass). The prefixes *milli* and *kilo* in front of a base unit help determine size.

milli = 1,000 times smaller than the base
kilo = 1,000 times larger than the base

Practice

Choose the units that would best measure each object.

____ 1. weight of a boy   A. kilometers
____ 2. capacity of a water tower B. grams
____ 3. liquid baby medicine   C. milliliters
____ 4. distance between two cities D. kiloliters
____ 5. length of a paperclip   E. milligrams
____ 6. large bottle of soda   F. liters
____ 7. weight of a paperclip   G. kilograms
____ 8. short distance race   H. meters
____ 9. weight of a banana   I. millimeters

Check Your Work

Look at each of your answers carefully. Did you choose the right type of measurement for each object? Did you choose the correct unit size for each object?

Name _____   Date _____

(MEASUREMENT)

CONVERTING CUSTOMARY LENGTHS

ERROR ALERT! Make sure you use the correct conversions.

12 inches = 1 foot
3 feet = 1 yard
5,280 feet = 1 mile

Problems: Find the equivalent measurements.

Sherika's Answers:

1. 7 yards = $2\frac{1}{3}$ feet
2. 24 inches = 2 feet
3. 6 feet = 18 yards
4. 10 miles = 52,800 feet
5. 60 inches = 5 feet

6. 30 feet = 10 yards
7. 3 feet = 48 inches
8. 4 yards = 12 feet
9. 2 miles = 2,640 feet
10. 4 inches = 12 feet

? Is That Correct?—Does the answer make sense?

Larissa checked Sherika's answer to problem 1. This is what she said.

"Does 7 yards = $2\frac{1}{3}$ feet? Feet are smaller than yards. So, it should take more feet to make up the same number of yards. The answer should be more than 7 feet, but it's not. This answer doesn't make sense."

For each problem, decide whether the number should get bigger or smaller. Put a checkmark next to any answers that are too big or too small.

Check each checkmarked answer carefully to find Sherika's mistake.

- Did she divide to convert from smaller units to bigger units?
- Did she multiply to convert from bigger units to smaller units?
- Did she multiply or divide by the correct amount? Correct any mistakes.

© McGraw-Hill Children's Publishing

0-7424-2783-8 *Is That Correct?*

Name _____ Date _____

<MEASUREMENT>

Converting Customary Lengths

Error Alert! Multiply to convert from bigger units to smaller units. Divide to convert from smaller units to bigger units. Make sure you use the correct conversions:

12 inches = 1 foot
3 feet = 1 yard
5,280 feet = 1 mile

Practice

Find the equivalent measurements.

1. 36 inches = _____ feet
2. 10 yards = _____ feet
3. 4 miles = _____ feet
4. 8 feet = _____ inches
5. 66 feet = _____ yards
6. 15,840 feet = _____ miles

7. 10 feet = _____ inches
8. 12 yards = _____ feet
9. 12 feet = _____ yards
10. 2 miles = _____ feet
11. 108 inches = _____ feet
12. 12 inches = _____ feet

Check Your Work

Check your work. Use the following checklist on each answer.
- Do the answers make sense?
- Did you divide to convert from smaller units to bigger units?
- Did you multiply to convert from bigger units to smaller units?
- Did you multiply or divide by the correct amount?

Name _____ Date _____

(MEASUREMENT)

CONVERTING METRIC LENGTHS

ERROR ALERT! Make sure you use the correct conversion factors.

10 millimeters (mm) = 1 centimeter (cm)
100 centimeters (cm) = 1 meter (m)
1,000 meters (m) = 1 kilometer (km)

Problems: Find the equivalent measurements.

Thien's Answers:

1. 20 m = <u>200 cm</u>
2. 5 km = <u>5,000 m</u>
3. 400 cm = <u>4 m</u>
4. 3,200 mm = <u>32 cm</u>

5. 75 m = <u>7,500 cm</u>
6. 400 cm = <u>4 mm</u>
7. 600 mm = <u>60 cm</u>
8. 50 km = <u>5 m</u>

Is That Correct?—Does the answer make sense?

Cho checked Thien's answer to problem 1. This is what she said:

"Could 20 meters = 200 cm? Centimeters are smaller than meters. So, it should take more centimeters to make up the same number of meters. The answer should be more than 20 feet, which it is."

For each problem, decide whether the number should get bigger or smaller. Put a checkmark next to any answers that are too big or too small.

Then Cho took a closer look at the answer.

"Converting from bigger units to smaller units means multiply. There are 100 centimeters in a meter. 20 × 100 = 2,000 The answer should be 2,000 cm, not 200 cm."

For each problem, make sure the correct conversion factor was used. Make sure there were no arithmetic errors. Correct any mistakes.

Name _____   Date _____

<Measurement>

Converting Metric Lengths

Error Alert! Make sure you use the correct conversion factors.

10 millimeters (mm) = 1 centimeter (cm)
100 centimeters (cm) = 1 meter (m)
1,000 meters (m) = 1 kilometer (km)

Practice

Find the equivalent measurements.

1. 40 m = _____ cm

2. 2 km = _____ m

3. 800 cm = _____ m

4. 5,320 mm = _____ cm

5. 62 m = _____ cm

6. 700 cm = _____ mm

7. 200 mm = _____ cm

8. 80 km = _____ m

9. 6 m = _____ cm

10. 900 cm = _____ m

11. 5 m = _____ cm

12. 8 cm = _____ mm

Check Your Work

Check your work. Use the following checklist on each answer.

- Do the answers make sense?
- Did you divide to convert from smaller units to bigger units?
- Did you multiply to convert from bigger units to smaller units?
- Did you multiply or divide by the correct amount?

© McGraw-Hill Children's Publishing   0-7424-2783-8 *Is That Correct?*

Name _____ Date _____

(MEASUREMENT)

Applications—Money

Problem: A box of magic tricks costs 65¢. Belia takes an even number of coins out of her pocket to pay for it. What coins could they be?

Consuela's Answer: 2 quarters and 15 pennies
Evita's Answer: 6 dimes and 1 nickel
Carmen's Answer: 2 quarters, 1 dime, and 1 nickel
Manuela's Answer: 5 dimes, 2 nickels, and 5 pennies
Julieta's Answer: 2 quarters and 2 dimes

Is That Correct?—Does the answer match the question?

1. Check to make sure the coins add up to the exact amount needed. Does Consuela's answer make 65¢? _____

    2 quarters = 25¢ + 25¢ = _____

    15 pennies = _____ ¢

    total amount = _____ + _____ = _____

2. Check to make sure all the other conditions in the problem are met. How many total coins did Consuela include in her answer? _____ Is this an even number? _____

3. Is Consuela's answer correct? _____

4. Check the other students' answers. Which of them have correct answers?

Practice

5. Sofia buys a poster for 70¢. She uses an odd number of coins to buy it. What coins could they be? Prove your answer is right.

6. A box of magnets costs 50¢. Paulita takes 10 coins out of her pocket to pay for it. What coins could they be? Prove your answer is right.

© McGraw-Hill Children's Publishing

0-7424-2783-8 Is That Correct?

Name _____ Date _____

<MEASUREMENT>

Applications—Money

Problem: Thaniel and Ty fed the horses at the fair. Their mother game them 3 one-dollar bills, 3 quarters, 5 dimes, and 3 nickels. The boys divided the money equally. What pieces of money did each of them get?

Jamarr's Answer: Thaniel gets 2 one-dollar bills, 2 dimes, and 3 nickels. Ty gets 1 one-dollar bill, 3 quarters, and 2 dimes. They both get 7 pieces of money.

Is That Correct?—Does the answer make sense?

1. What do you think "they divided the money equally" means?

2. Do you think Jamarr's answer is correct? Why or why not?

3. How would you have answered this question?

Practice

4. Leon and Shawn washed cars one Saturday. When they finished, they had 3 one-dollar bills, 1 half dollar, 3 quarters, 2 dimes, and 1 nickel. The boys divided the money fairly. What pieces of money did each of them get? Prove your answer is right.

5. Rashon and Kordell went to the video arcade. Their mother gave them 5 one-dollar bills, 7 quarters, 1 half dollar, 5 dimes, and 1 nickel. The boys divided the money equally. What pieces of money did each of them get? Prove your answer is right.

Name _____ Date _____

(MEASUREMENT)

Applications—Time

Problem: The bell rings for recess to begin at 12:15 P.M. and rings again at 1:00 P.M. for recess to end. Tamika volunteers to help her teacher water the classroom plants for the first 10 minutes of recess. How many minutes will she have left to play kickball when she is finished?

Nisha's Answer: Tamika will have 35 minutes left to play kickball.

Is That Correct?—Put the answer back into the problem.

1. Recess begins at 12:15 P.M. Tamika waters the plants for 10 minutes. What time is it now? _____

2. Then Tamika plays kickball for 35 minutes, until recess ends. What time is it now? _____

3. Is Nisha's answer correct? _____

Practice

4. Music class is every Thursday at 1:30 P.M. The students stay for 1 hour and 15 minutes. If warm up and practice takes 45 minutes, how much time will they have left to learn a new song?

5. The bus leaves at 10:05 A.M. and arrives at the museum at 11:20 A.M. The bus traveled on the highway for 55 minutes. How much time did the bus travel off the highway?

Check Your Work

Check to make sure the times are correct. Put your answers back into the problems. Correct any mistakes.

© McGraw-Hill Children's Publishing   0-7424-2783-8 *Is That Correct?*

Name _____ Date _____

<MEASUREMENT>

Applications—Time

Problem: Patrick told Rick he would be at his house at 4:05 P.M. It takes 15 minutes to bike there. He left his house at 3:55 P.M. Will Patrick be early, on time, or late? By how many minutes?

Blake's Answer: Patrick will be exactly on time.

Check Your Work—Use a model.

1. Use the clock face. Use a colored pencil to draw hands on the clock showing 3:55.

2. Use a different colored pencil to draw hands on the clock showing 4:05.

3. Use the clock face to count by 5s to find the number of minutes between 3:55 and 4:05. How many minutes elapsed? _____

4. Is Blake's answer correct? Did Patrick make it on time? _____ If not, what should the correct answer be? _____

Practice

5. Garrett needs to arrive at school at 8:10 A.M. It takes him 20 minutes to walk. What is the latest time he could leave his house? _____

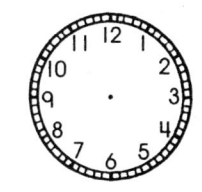

6. Victor's baseball game starts at 6:15 P.M. The game lasts 1 hour. His family plans to go out for ice cream afterwards. Ice cream and the trip home take 35 minutes. What time will Victor get home? _____

Check Your Work

Check your answers. Use the clock faces to model the problems.

© McGraw-Hill Children's Publishing

0-7424-2783-8 *Is That Correct?*

Name _____ Date _____

(MEASUREMENT)

Applications—Temperature

ERROR ALERT! The following formulas give a good estimate of the conversion between Celsius and Fahrenheit temperatures between 32 and 95 degrees Fahrenheit:

Celsius to Fahrenheit: Double the Celsius temperature and then add 30.
Fahrenheit to Celsius: Subtract 30 and then divide by 2.

Problem: The temperature outside is 30 degrees Celsius. What is the approximate temperature in degrees Fahrenheit?

Molly's Answer: The temperature is 10 degrees Fahrenheit.

Is That Correct?—Does the answer make sense?

1. Water freezes at 0 degrees Celsius and 32 degrees Fahrenheit. Will the numbers in the Fahrenheit scale be higher or lower than the numbers in the Celsius scale? _____

2. Does Molly's answer make sense? _____ Why or why not?

Check Your Work—Use a formula.

3. Find the correct answer to the problem. Show your work.

4. Explain to Molly why your answer makes more sense than hers.

Name _____ Date _____

<MEASUREMENT>

Applications—Temperature

ERROR ALERT! The following formulas give a good estimate of the conversion between Celsius and Fahrenheit temperatures between 32 and 95 degrees Fahrenheit:

Celsius to Fahrenheit: Double the Celsius temperature and then add 30.
Fahrenheit to Celsius: Subtract 30 and then divide by 2.

Practice

1. The temperature in the room is 20 degrees Celsius. What is the temperature in degrees Fahrenheit? Show your work.

2. The temperature outside is 27 degrees Celsius. Would you be more likely to go swimming or skiing? Explain your answer.

3. It is a hot day in July. The Fahrenheit temperature is 80 degrees. What is the Celsius temperature? Show your work.

4. The temperature is 40 degrees Fahrenheit. What is the Celsius temperature? Show your work.

Check Your Work

Go over each answer carefully using the following checklist.

- Does the answer make sense?
- Did you use the correct formula?
- Check your arithmetic.

Name _____   Date _____

(DATA ANALYSIS AND PROBABILITY)

How Likely?

Problems: For each event, decide if the outcome is certain, likely, unlikely, or impossible.

Armando's Answers:

A. You will win the lottery tomorrow.   unlikely
B. Someone you know will win the million-dollar lottery tomorrow.   unlikely
C. Independence Day is celebrated in July.   certain
D. It will rain next Tuesday.   likely
E. All students will be absent from class tomorrow.   certain
F. All students will be present in class tomorrow.   impossible

Is That Correct?—Consider the point of view.

1. Are Armando's answers correct? How do you know?

2. Enrique is in the same third-grade class as Armando. He disagreed with Armando's answer to **A**. He thinks the event is impossible. But, he agrees with Armando's answer to **B**. Explain Enrique's thinking.

3. Armando's friend Lorenzo lives in another state. His answer to **D** was unlikely. How could both students be correct?

4. Enrique answered the questions 3 days after Armando. His answer to **E** was unlikely. How could both students be correct?

5. Look at Armando's answer to **C**. Could someone else answer this differently and still be correct? Explain.

© McGraw-Hill Children's Publishing

0-7424-2783-8 Is That Correct?

Name _____ Date _____

<Data Analysis and Probability>

Equally Likely?

Error Alert! Two events are equally likely only if they have the exact same chance of happening.

Problem: There are 3 red cubes, 3 green cubes, 2 blue cubes, and 2 yellow cubes in a bag. A cube is randomly drawn from the bag. Which of the following pairs of outcomes are equally likely?

   A. red and blue   **B.** red and green
   C. blue and green   **D.** blue and yellow

Ayita's Answer: B

Is That Correct?—Consider all answer choices.

1. Look at choice **B**. How many red cubes are in the bag? _____ How many green cubes are in the bag? _____ Is the chance of drawing a green cube the same as drawing a red cube? _____

2. Is Ayita's answer correct? _____

3. Look at choice **A**. How many red cubes are in the bag? _____ How many blue cubes are in the bag? _____ Is the chance of drawing a blue cube the same as drawing a red cube? _____

4. Look at choice **C**. How many blue cubes are in the bag? _____ How many green cubes are in the bag? _____ Is the chance of drawing a green cube the same as drawing a blue cube? _____

5. Look at choice **D**. How many blue cubes are in the bag? _____ How many yellow cubes are in the bag? _____ Is the chance of drawing a blue cube the same as drawing a yellow cube? _____

6. Is Ayita's answer complete? _____

© McGraw-Hill Children's Publishing

0-7424-2783-8 *Is That Correct?*

Name _____ Date _____

(DATA ANALYSIS AND PROBABILITY)

Equally Likely?

ERROR ALERT! Two events are equally likely only if they have the exact same chance of happening.

Problem: Which outcomes on the spinner are equally likely?

Kele's Answer: The numbers 1, 2, and 3 are all equally likely since each number only appears once.

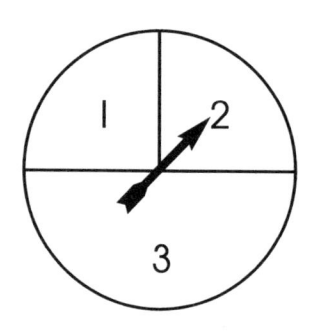

Check Your Work—Use the correct process.

1. Does each number only appear once on the spinner? _____

2. Does this mean the spinner has the same chance of landing on each number? _____

3. Explain to Kele why his answer is incorrect.

4. What should the correct answer be? _____

Practice

For each spinner, will the outcomes of 1 and 2 be equally likely? How do you know?

5.

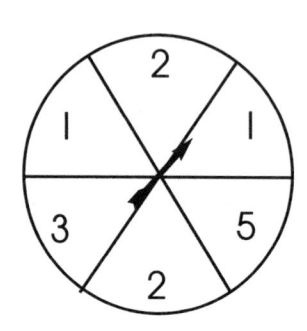

6.

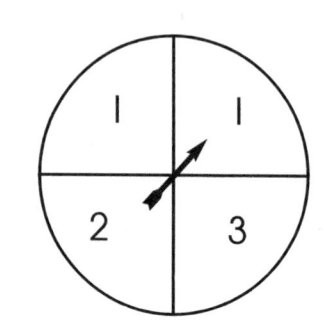

7.

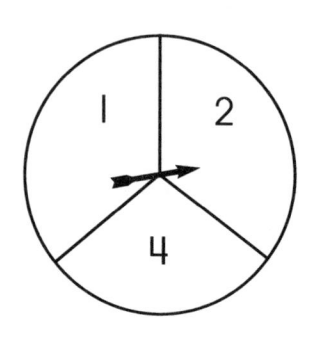

© McGraw-Hill Children's Publishing

0-7424-2783-8 *Is That Correct?*

Name _____ Date _____

<Data Analysis and Probability>

Probability

Problem: Dallen put 2 red cubes, 1 blue cube, and 3 purple cubes in a bag. If he randomly pulls a cube out of the bag, what is his chance of getting a red cube? Blue? Purple?

Carnell's Answers: Red: $\frac{2}{4}$ Blue: $\frac{1}{5}$ Purple: $\frac{3}{3}$

Hareem's Answers: Red: $\frac{4}{2}$ Blue: $\frac{5}{1}$ Purple: $\frac{3}{3}$

Jeffon's Answers: Red: $\frac{2}{6}$ Blue: $\frac{1}{6}$ Purple: $\frac{3}{6}$

Kenton's Answers: Red: $\frac{6}{2}$ Blue: $\frac{6}{1}$ Purple: $\frac{6}{3}$

Check Your Work—Use the correct definition.

The numerator (top number) tells you how many items have that characteristic. The denominator (bottom number) tells you how many total items there are.

1. Which number should be larger, the numerator or the denominator? Based on this, whose answers are incorrect?

2. If the chance of drawing red is $\frac{2}{4}$, then there are _____ red cubes and _____ total cubes. Does this match the information in the problem? _____

3. If the chance of drawing blue is $\frac{1}{6}$, then there is _____ blue cube and _____ total cubes. Does this match the information in the problem? _____

4. Check each student's answers. Who has the correct answers?

5. Look at Carnell's answers. How do you think he got his answers? What would you tell Carnell?

Name _____   Date _____

(DATA ANALYSIS AND PROBABILITY)

Probability

ERROR ALERT! The chance that an event happens is the number of ways it could happen out of the total number of possibilities.

Problem: Anica and Carlota are playing a board game. Each student throws 2 dice when it is her turn to move. Anica needs to roll a sum of 7 to land on the last square and win the game. Carlota needs to roll a sum of 9 to win. Does either student have a better chance of winning?

Elsa's Answer: Both students have the same chance of winning. The dice are fair, and each number has the same chance of being rolled.

Check Your Work—Use a model.

Check Elsa's answer. Draw models of the situation to find the chance of rolling each sum.

1. Here are two ways Anica could roll a 7:

   Draw all the other ways Anica could roll a 7. How many ways are there to roll a 7? _____

2. There are 36 total possible dice combinations. What is the chance of rolling a sum of 7? _____

3. Draw all the ways Carlota could roll a 9. How many ways are there to roll a sum of 9? _____

4. What is the probability of rolling a 9? _____

5. Was Elsa's answer correct? Explain.

© McGraw-Hill Children's Publishing

0-7424-2783-8 *Is That Correct?*

Name _____ Date _____

<Data Analysis and Probability>

Probability

Practice

Look at the spinner. What is the chance the arrow will land on each of the following:

1. a number? _____
2. an 8? _____
3. a circle? _____
4. a shape? _____
5. a triangle? _____

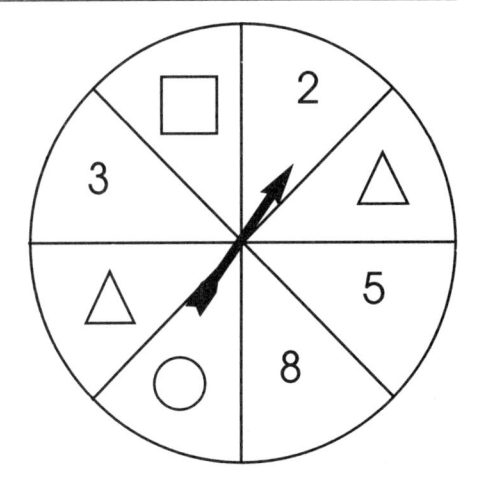

Look at the spinner. What is the chance the arrow will land on each of the following:

6. a 5? _____
7. an odd number? _____
8. a triangle? _____
9. a 2? _____
10. a shape _____

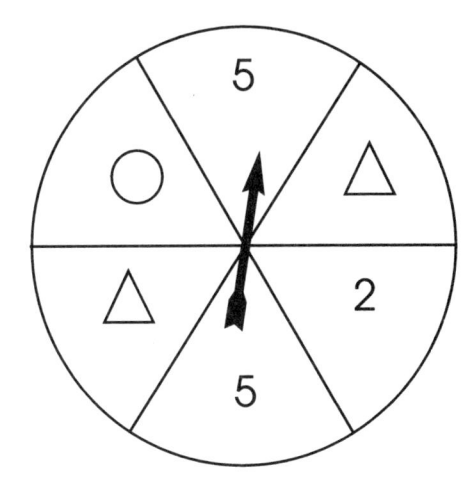

Check Your Work

Check each of your answers using the following checklist.

- The number in the denominator is the same as the total number of equal parts on the spinner.
- The number in the numerator is the same as the number of parts that have the chosen characteristic.

© McGraw-Hill Children's Publishing

0-7424-2783-8 *Is That Correct?*

Name _____ Date _____

(Data Analysis and Probability)

RANGE

Problem: Find the minimum and maximum number of books read by each class. Then find the range in the number of books read by each class.

Teacher	Number of books read by each student
Mrs. Rodriguez:	5, 1, 3, 2, 7, 10, 1, 3, 5, 1, 4, 3, 6, 5, 1, 2, 4
Mr. Mohammed:	3, 3, 3, 4, 6, 4, 3, 5, 2, 3, 3, 4, 5, 6, 4, 3
Ms. Chin:	8, 3, 1, 4, 5, 2, 7, 6, 2, 4, 3, 1, 3, 5, 8, 0, 2, 4
Miss Rogers:	3, 1, 2, 0, 2, 3, 1, 3, 4, 6, 5, 5, 3, 2, 7, 4, 6

Nicole's Answers:

	Minimum	Maximum	Range
Mrs. Rodriguez:	1	10	9
Mr. Mohammed:	3	6	3
Ms. Chin:	1	8	7
Miss Rogers:	0	6	6

Is That Correct?—Know the correct definition.

The range is the difference between the highest (maximum) and lowest (minimum) values.

1. Look at Nicole's answers for Mrs. Rodriguez's class. Subtract the maximum value by the minimum value to find the range. Did Nicole calculate the range correctly? _____

2. Now look at the data for Mr. Mohammed's class. Did Nicole choose the correct minimum and maximum values? _____ How will this change the range? _____

3. Check Nicole's answers for each class. Cross out any wrong answers and write the correct answer next to it.

© McGraw-Hill Children's Publishing

0-7424-2783-8 *Is That Correct?*

Name _____ Date _____

<Data Analysis and Probability>

Mode

Problem: Find the mode number of books read by each class.

Teacher	Number of books read by each student
Mrs. Rodriguez:	5, 1, 3, 2, 7, 10, 1, 3, 5, 1, 4, 3, 6, 5, 1, 2, 4
Mr. Mohammed:	3, 3, 3, 4, 6, 4, 3, 5, 2, 4, 3, 4, 5, 6, 4, 3
Ms. Chin:	8, 3, 2, 4, 5, 2, 7, 6, 2, 4, 3, 1, 3, 5, 8, 0, 2, 4

Is That Correct?—Know the correct definition.

A group of students were given the problem above. They split up the work. Each boy found the mode for a different class and explained how he found it to the others. Read each student's answer and explanation.

Anh's Answer: Mrs. Rodriguez's class: mode = 3.7
  "I added all the values, which was 63. Then I used a calculator to divide by the number of students, 17. The answer was 3.7."

Aidan's Answer: Mr. Muhammed's class: mode = 4
  "I put the numbers in order from lowest to highest. Then I found the middle number, which was 4."

Benito's Answer: Ms. Chin's class: mode = 2
  "I found the value that occurred most often. There were more 2s than any other number."

1. Which student used the correct definition of mode?

2. Was his answer correct?

3. Use the correct definition of mode to correct any mistakes made by the students. Show your work on the back of this page. Write the correct mode for each class below.

   Mrs. Rodriguez: _____   Ms. Chin: _____

   Mr. Monammed: _____

© McGraw-Hill Children's Publishing   0-7424-2783-8 Is That Correct?

Name _____ Date _____
(Data Analysis and Probability)

Median

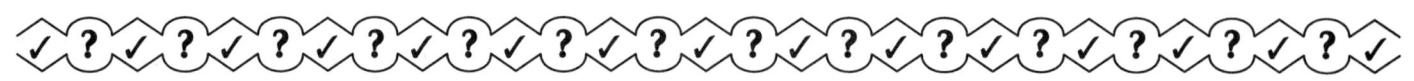

Problem: Find the median number of books read by each class.

Teacher	Number of books read by each student
Mrs. Rodriguez:	5, 1, 3, 2, 7, 10, 1, 3, 5, 1, 4, 3, 6, 5, 1, 2, 4
Mr. Mohammed:	3, 3, 3, 4, 6, 4, 3, 5, 2, 4, 3, 4, 5, 6, 4, 3
Ms. Chin:	8, 3, 2, 4, 5, 2, 7, 6, 2, 4, 3, 1, 3, 5, 8, 0, 2, 4

Is That Correct?—Know the correct definition.

A group of students were given the problem above. They split up the work. Each boy found the median for a different class and explained how he found it to the others. Read each student's answer and explanation.

Anh's Answer: Mrs. Rodriguez's class: median = 3.7
  "I added all the values, which was 63. Then I used a calculator to divide by the number of students, 17. The answer was 3.7."

Aidan's Answer: Mr. Muhammed's class: median = 4
  "I put the numbers in order from lowest to highest. Then I found the middle number, which was 4."

Benito's Answer: Ms. Chin's class: median = 2
  "I found the value that occurred most often. There were more 2s than any other number."

1. Which student used the correct definition of median? _____

2. Did he calculate the answer correctly? _____

3. Use the correct definition of median to correct any mistakes made by the students. Show your work on the back of this page. Write the correct median for each class below.

   Mrs. Rodriguez: _____   Ms. Chin: _____

   Mr. Mohammed: _____

Name _____   Date _____

<Data Analysis and Probability>

MEAN

Problem: Find the mean number of books read by each class.

Teacher	Number of books read by each student
Mrs. Rodriguez:	5, 1, 3, 2, 7, 10, 1, 3, 5, 1, 4, 3, 6, 5, 1, 2, 4
Mr. Mohammed:	3, 3, 3, 4, 6, 4, 3, 5, 2, 4, 3, 4, 5, 6, 4, 3
Ms. Chin:	8, 3, 2, 4, 5, 2, 7, 6, 2, 4, 3, 1, 3, 5, 8, 0, 2, 4

Is That Correct?—Know the correct definition.

A group of students were given the problem above. They split up the work. Each boy found the mean for a different class and explained how he found it to the others. Read each student's answer and explanation.

Anh's Answer: Mrs. Rodriguez's class: mean = 3.7
   "I added all the values, which was 63. Then I used a calculator to divide by the number of students, 17. The answer was 3.7."

Aidan's Answer: Mr. Muhammed's class: mean = 4
   "I put the numbers in order from lowest to highest. Then I found the middle number, which was 4."

Benito's Answer: Ms. Chin's class: mean = 2
   "I found the value that occurred most often. There were more 2s than any other number."

1. Which student used the correct definition of mean? _____

2. Did he calculate the answer correctly? _____

3. Use the correct definition of mean to correct any mistakes made by the students. Show your work on the back of this page. Write the correct mean for each class below.

   Mrs. Rodriguez: _____   Ms. Chin: _____

   Mr. Mohammed: _____

© McGraw-Hill Children's Publishing

Name _____ Date _____

(Data Analysis and Probability)

Applications—Interpreting Data

Practice

Kayleigh had a very good year playing basketball. The following data shows the number of points she scored per game during February and March.

22, 25, 31, 27, 24, 29, 24

Calculate the summary statistic (mean, median, mode, or range) that best completes each statement. Tell which statistic you used.

1. The number of points Kayleigh scored varied by ____ points per game.

    summary statistic: _____ = _____

2. On average, Kayleigh scored ____ points per game.

    summary statistic: _____ = _____

3. Kayleigh scored more than ____ points in half of her games.

    summary statistic: _____ = _____

4. Most often, Kayleigh scored ____ points per game.

    summary statistic: _____ = _____

Check Your Work

Check each of your answers. Circle the clue word in the question that helped you decide which summary statistic to choose. Look up the definition of that summary statistic. How does the clue word relate to the definition?

Name _____ Date _____

<Data Analysis and Probability>

Applications—Interpreting Data

Practice

Ms. Snider's science class went on a nature walk. The following data shows the number of different types of leaves each student found for his or her scrapbook.

7, 7, 8, 9, 9, 9, 10, 10, 11, 11, 11, 12, 12, 12, 12, 12, 13, 13, 14, 18

Calculate the summary statistic (mean, median, mode, or range) that best completes each statement. Tell which statistic you used.

1. The number of leaves collected the most was _____.

   summary statistic: _____ = _____

2. On average, each student collected _____ leaves.

   summary statistic: _____ = _____

3. The number of leaves collected varied by _____.

   summary statistic: _____ = _____

4. Half the children collected more than _____ leaves.

   summary statistic: _____ = _____

Check Your Work

Check each of your answers. Circle the clue word in the question that helped you decide which summary statistic to choose. Look up the definition of that summary statistic. How does the clue word relate to the definition?

Applications—Tally Charts

(Data Analysis and Probability)

Problem: The crossing guards are concerned that so many cars cross a street they do not monitor. They are using a tally chart to help present their findings to the principal. Look at the tally chart. How many cars were on Johnson Avenue each day?

Day	Number of Cars
Monday	|||| |||| |||| ||||
Tuesday	|||| |||| ||||	
Wednesday	|||| |||| |||| |||| ||
Thursday	|||| |||| ||||
Friday	|||| |||| |||| |||| |||| ||||

Diego's Answers:

Day	Number of Cars
Monday	19
Tuesday	21
Wednesdy	22
Thursday	9
Friday	24

Check Your Work—Use the correct process.

1. What does a group of tally marks with a diagonal slash through it represent?

2. How do you count each group of tally marks?

3. How do you count the tally marks without a diagonal slash?

4. Count the tally marks for each day carefully. Correct any answers Diego may have gotten wrong.

Name _____ Date _____

<Data Analysis and Probability>

Applications—Tally Charts

⊙ Practice

Akilah went on a walk through the park. She kept a tally of each kind of wild animal she saw. Use her tally chart to answer the questions.

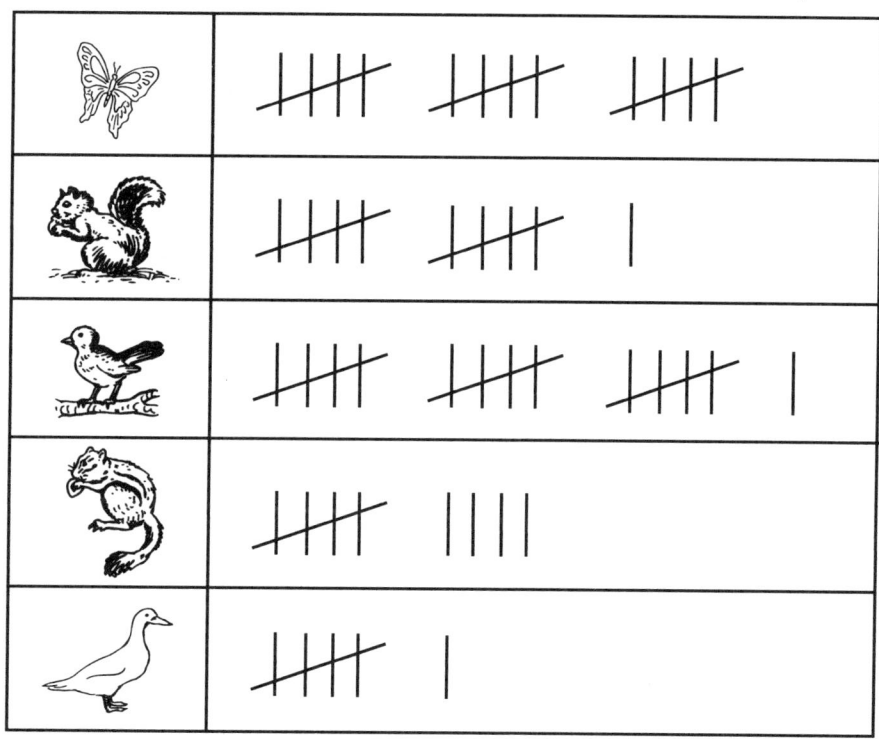

Animal	Tally
butterfly	|||| |||| ||||
squirrel	|||| ||||	
bird	|||| |||| ||||	
chipmunk	|||| ||||
duck	||||	

1. Which animal did Akilah spot 11 times? _____

2. Which animal did Akilah see the most? _____
   How many times was it seen? _____

3. Which animal did Akilah see the least? _____
   How many times was it seen? _____

4. How many chipmunks did Akilah see? _____

5. How many butterflies did Akilah see? _____

✓ Check Your Work

Trade papers with a classmate. Check his or her answers.

© McGraw-Hill Children's Publishing   0-7424-2783-8 *Is That Correct?*

Applications—Line Plots

Problem: The *Shop 'N Save* just opened for business. The manager kept track of how many customers came each day of the first week. The data is shown in the graph.

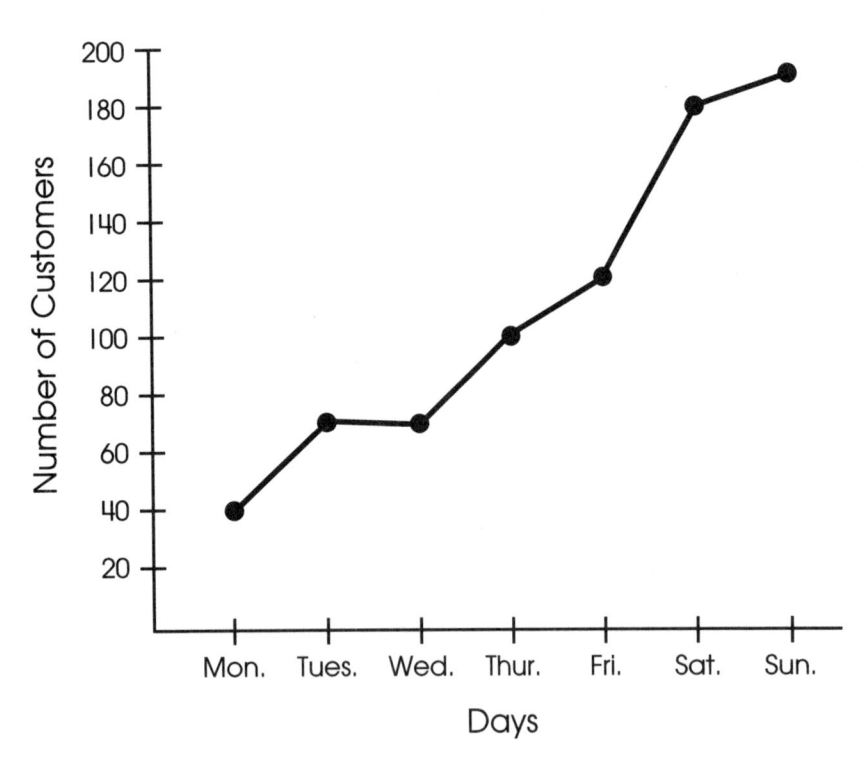

Between which 2 days did the number of customers increase the most? The least? Between which 2 days did the number of customers stay the same?

Jim's Answer: The number of customers increased the most between Friday and Saturday. It changed the the least between Thursday and Friday. It didn't change at all between Tuesday and Wednesday.

Check Your Work

1. Use the graph to make a table showing the number of customers each day.

Day	Mon.	Tues.	Wed.	Thur.	Fri.	Sat.	Sun.
Customers							

2. Find the change in the number of customers from one day to the next.

   Mon.-Tues. _____   Tues.-Wed. _____   Wed.-Thurs. _____

   Thur.-Fri. _____   Fri.-Sat. _____   Sat.-Sun. _____

3. Look at Jim's answer. Was he correct? If not, correct his mistakes.

Name _____ Date _____

(DATA ANALYSIS AND PROBABILITY)

Applications—Bar Graphs

Problems: The following bar graph shows sports played by third-grade students at Cooper Elementary.

Sports Played by Third Graders

A. Which sport is played by the most students?

B. Which sport is played by the the least students?

C. How many more students play baseball than football?

D. How many more students play volleyball than baseball?

Calida's Answers:

A. soccer

B. football

C. 2

D. 4

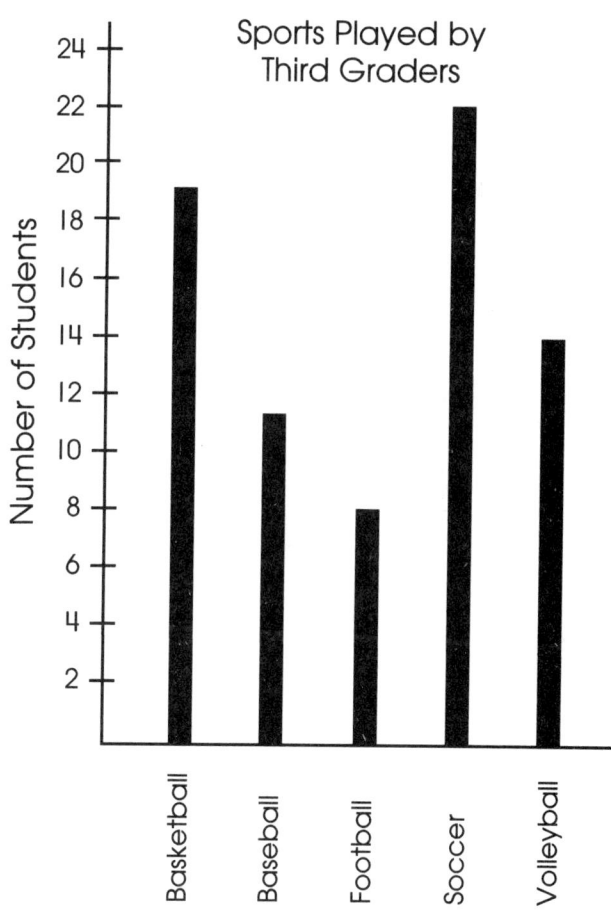

1. How could a ruler or a straight-edge help you make sure you read the graph correctly?

2. What does it mean if a bar ends halfway between two numbers?

3. How many students play each sport?

   basketball _____   football _____   soccer _____   volleyball _____

4. Use your answers from problem **3** to check Calida's answers. Correct any answers that are wrong.

Name _____ Date _____

<Data Analysis and Probability>

Applications—Bar Graphs

Problem: The following data was collected from two third-grade classrooms. Make a bar graph of the data.

Vishon's Answer:

Ways to School

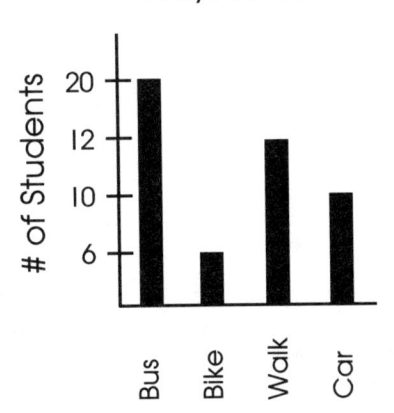

Ways to School	# of Students
(bus)	20
(bike)	6
(walk)	12
(car)	10

1. Look at the table. What is the difference between the number of students who ride the bus and those who walk? _____

2. Look at the table. What is the difference between the number of students who walk and those who ride in cars? _____

3. Which difference is greater, that between the bus and walking, or that between walking and cars? _____

4. Look at the graph. Look at the distance from the top of the bus bar to the top of the walk bar. Compare that to the distance from the top of the walk bar to the top of the car bar. How do the distances compare?

5. Do you think Vishon's graph is accurate? Why or why not?

© McGraw-Hill Children's Publishing   0-7424-2783-8 *Is That Correct?*

Answer Key

Rounding Numbers 5
1. hundred; ten; no; no
2. yes; no; Mary just made all the last digits 0. She didn't ever round up.
3. A. 220; B. 130; C. 560; D. 680
4. 900
5. 700
6. 1,900
7. 21,500

Composing Numbers 6
1. more; Numbers are being added to 10,000, so the answer should be more than 10,000.
2. Jerome's; He put the 1 for 10,000 in the thousands place instead of the ten thousands place. He did not put a zero in the thousands place.
3. No; four thousands = 4,000; zero hundreds = 0; six tens = 60; 8 ones = 8
4. 10,468; Darnel put the 4 for 400 in the thousands place instead of the hundreds place. He put a zero in the hundreds place instead of the thousands place.
5. 421,026
6. 300,278

Decomposing Numbers 7
1. Possible answer: Deshawna's number is not large enough. Her largest number is 1,000, but the original number is over 10,000.
2. No; 12,570
3. Kineisha is correct.
4. 7,000 + 200 + 10 + 6
5. 200,000 + 4,000 + 100 + 20 + 5
6. 600,000 + 10,000 + 6,000

Comparing Whole Numbers 8
1. correct
2. correct
3. incorrect
4. correct
5. correct
6. incorrect
7. incorrect
8. correct
9. correct

Comparing Whole Numbers 9
1. <
2. <
3. >
4. <
5. <
6. >
7. >
8. >
9. <
10. >
11. >
12. <
13. >
14. <
15. >
16. >

Comparing Decimals 10
1. correct
2. incorrect
3. correct
4. correct
5. correct
6. incorrect
7. correct
8. correct
9. correct

Comparing Decimals 11
1. <
2. <
3. >
4. <
5. <
6. >
7. <
8. >
9. <
10. <
11. >
12. <
13. >
14. =
15. >
16. >

Ordering Whole Numbers 12
1. Madison listed the numbers from greatest to least, not from least to greatest.
2. No. 2,514 is greater than 2,415, so these should be switched.
3. 2,045; 2,405; 2,415; 2,451; 2,514; 2,541
4. 678; 789; 798; 799; 800; 1,000
5. 1,023; 1,032; 1,203; 1,204; 1,320; 1,432
6. 21,417; 21,471; 24,127; 24,712; 27,214; 27,412

Ordering Decimals 13
1. José is thinking about whole numbers, where more digits in the number means it's a higher number. This is not true when comparing decimals.
2. Yes, everything Juan said was correct.
3. No. Juan was so focused on looking at the numbers after the decimal point that he forgot to look at the numbers in front of the decimal point. So, he put 6.2 in front of 5.4, even though 6 is larger than 5.
4. Possible answer: First, look at the number in front of the decimal. Put all the numbers starting with a 4 before numbers starting with a 5 and all numbers starting with a 5 before numbers starting with a 6. If the number before the decimal is the same, then compare the digits after the decimal. Add zero(s) to the end of the numbers so they all have the same place value. Then compare the decimal numbers and put the numbers in order.
4.61, 4.9, 5.4, 5.49, 6.12, 6.2

Parts of a Whole 14
1. no
2. The numerator and denominator numbers are switched.
3. No.
4. Kwan's answers represent the dotted part of each figure.
5. A. $\frac{2}{3}$ B. $\frac{1}{4}$ C. $\frac{2}{9}$ D. $\frac{2}{6}$

Parts of a Whole 15
1. dotted = $\frac{2}{7}$; shaded = $\frac{4}{7}$; white = $\frac{1}{7}$
2. dotted = 0; shaded = $\frac{1}{3}$; white = $\frac{2}{3}$
3. dotted = $\frac{1}{5}$; shaded = $\frac{2}{5}$; white = $\frac{2}{5}$
4. dotted = $\frac{5}{8}$; shaded = $\frac{2}{8}$; white = $\frac{1}{8}$

Parts of a Set 16
1. Davonn used a 2 for 2 broken vases and a 4 for 4 whole vases. He did not use the right numerator or denominator.
2. Keishawn used a 4 for whole broken vases and a 2 for 2 broken vases. He did not use the right numerator or denominator.
3. Lamarr and Jamal
4. Jamal's
5. Lamarr wrote the fraction for the whole vases instead of the broken vases.

Parts of a Set 17
1. $\frac{2}{3}$
2. $\frac{3}{7}$
3. $\frac{1}{4}$
4. $\frac{4}{5}$
5. $\frac{2}{6}$

Comparing Fractions 18
1. correct
2. incorrect
3. incorrect
4. correct
5. incorrect
6. correct
7. correct
8. correct
9. incorrect
10. correct
11. incorrect
12. incorrect

Comparing Fractions 19
1. >
2. <
3. >
4. <
5. <
6. >
7. <
8. >
9. <

© McGraw-Hill Children's Publishing

0-7424-2783-8 *Is That Correct?*

Answer Key

Equivalent Fractions 20
1. no; yes
2. The numerator and denominator mean different things. Adding the same number to both doesn't make sense.
3. Check students' models. Yes.

Equivalent Fractions 21
1. 2/4
2. 4/8
3. 6/9
4. 6/8
5. 3/12
6. 3/6

Adding Fractions 22
1. 3; 2; 2/3
2. no
3. Add the numerators together. Keep the denominator the same.
4. 3/4
5. 3/5
6. 5/8

Subtracting Fractions 23
1. correct
2. 3/5
3. correct
4. 2/4
5. 5/11
6. correct
7. 4/11
8. correct

Adding Whole Numbers 24
1. no
2. She forgot to carry the 1.
3. 373
4. 833
5. 737

Adding Whole Numbers 25
1. 570 + 300 = 870; Trayvon's answer is off by 100, so it's not correct.
2. He forgot to add in the carried one above the hundreds place.
3. 1,113
4. 823
5. 511

Adding Whole Numbers 26
1. 4,679 = 4,000 + 600 + 70 + 9; 3,371 = 3,000 + 300 + 70 + 1; (4,000 + 3,000) + (600 + 300) + (70 + 70) + (9 + 1) = 7,000 + 900 + 140 + 10 = 8,050
2. yes
3. 7,740
4. 4,213
5. 6,739
6. 8,921

Adding Whole Numbers 27
1. 641
2. 736
3. 971
4. 804
5. 706
6. 1,010
7. 774
8. 484
9. 537
10. 6,191
11. 6,318
12. 7,614

Subtracting Whole Numbers 28
1. 27; Jorgé's answer wasn't correct.
2. In the ones column, he subtracted 5-2 instead of 2-3. He should have borrowed from the tens column.
3. 27
4. 17

Subtracting Whole Numbers 29
1. 500 - 100 = 400; Leticia's answer is closer to 500 than 400, so her answer may be wrong.
2. Leticia borrowed from the hundreds column, but forgot to cross out the 5 and make it a 4.
3. 222
4. 671
5. 103

Subtracting Whole Numbers 30
1. 1,419 + 1,143 = 2,562
2. yes; He worked the problem backwards and the numbers matched.
3. 2,906
4. 1,295
5. 1,091
6. 4,267
7. 2,194
8. 1,570

Subtracting Whole Numbers 31
1. 484
2. 355
3. 289
4. 579
5. 272
6. 288
7. 269
8. 357
9. 406

Mixing Addition and Subtraction 32
1. 620
2. 521
3. 506
4. 314
5. 539
6. 136
7. 254
8. 480
9. 251

Mixing Addition and Subtraction 33
1. 607
2. 782
3. 453
4. 214
5. 206
6. 3,188
7. 5,187
8. 4,893
9. 12,989

Adding and Subtracting Decimals 34
1. 0.3
2. correct
3. correct
4. 16.71
5. correct
6. 0.84
7. correct
8. 3.19
9. correct
10. correct
11. correct
12. 118.01
13. correct
14. 23.95

Adding and Subtracting Decimals 35
1. 21.71
2. 12.9
3. 1.8
4. 58.4
5. 67.49
6. 11.45
7. 23.32
8. 124.2
9. 41.49
10. 82.03

Multiplication 36
1. correct
2. 178
3. 285
4. correct
5. correct
6. 234

Multiplication 37
1. 180
2. 174
3. correct
4. correct
5. correct
6. 68
7. correct
8. 315

Multiplication 38
1. 1,664
2. 1,908
3. 758
4. 6,471
5. 1,176
6. 5,704
7. 1,314
8. 1,185
9. 735

Multiplication 39
1. 2,538
2. 2,205
3. 7,353
4. 1,625
5. 2,528
6. 1,956
7. 2,492
8. 1,617
9. 2,061

Division 40
1. 4; no
2. 6
3. 7
4. 7
5. 4
6. 3

Division 41
1. 4; 2
2. no
3. no; 21; 9
4. The remainder is larger than the divisor.
5. Her remainder was too large. She could have made one more group of 7.

Division 42
1. yes; 8 x 8 = 64; 64 + 2 = 66
2. Answers may vary.
3. 8 R2
4. 7 R6
5. 6 R3
6. 5 R1
7. 5 R1
8. 5 R7
9. 6 R2
10. 6 R5
11. 6 R1
12. 5 R3
13. 3 R3
14. 6 R2

© McGraw-Hill Children's Publishing

0-7424-2783-8 Is That Correct?

Answer Key

Division 43
1. 9 2. 7 3. 10
4. 9 5. 7 6. 7
7. 9 R1 8. 3 R8 9. 8 R2
10. 5 R4 11. 5 R5 12. 5 R2

Multiplication and Division 44
1. 644 2. 9 3. 304
4. 4,096 5. 12 6. 3,735
7. 6 R4 8. 1,766 9. 4 R5

Multiplication and Division 45
1. 252 2. 6 3. 132
4. 1,080 5. 18 6. 6,027
7. 4 R4 8. 2,829 9. 3 R5

Riddles 46
1. yes
2. yes
3. yes
4. no; 2 is an even digit
5. no
6. 1,300
7. 713
8. 4,646

Applications—Addition and Subtraction 47
1. yes; total
2. no; answer should be 1,054
3. 95 CDs
4. 1,419 customers

Applications—Addition and Subtraction 48
1. 15
2. 5 people; He forgot to include the 3 family members in the line.
3. $15
4. $0.20

Applications—Multiplication 49
1. yes; The word "each" is a clue to multiply.
2. yes
3. 120 fiction books
4. 60 picture books
5. 36 tables

Applications—Division 50
1. yes
2. 6; No, it's 2 meals short.
3. Jeremy forgot to include the remainder.
4. more accurate; Mark included the remainder of 2 meals in his answer.

Applications—Multiplication and Division 51
1. 4; 4
2. 102 moose
3. Seven of the groups will have 10 people each. The 8th group will have 9 people.
4. 35 people

Patterns 52
1. yes
2. Yukio; He added incorrectly.
3. You might make an arithmetic mistake.
4. 495, 594, 693; Rule: +99
5. 28, 25, 22; Rule: −3
6. 55, 40, 25; Rule: −15

Patterns 53
1. Answers will vary.
2. no
3. no
4. 37, 60, 97; Add the previous two numbers to get the next number.
5. 27, 34, 42; Add one more each time (+2, +3, +4, +5...)

Patterns 54
1. They both chose the same 3 terms. Their rules look different.
2. Yes, they both do. Both their rules work. Adding the same number again is the same as multiplying by 2.
3. 108, 324, 972; Rule: ×3
4. correct
5. correct
6. 80, 20, 5; Rule: ÷4
7. 24, 48, 96; Rule: ×2
8. 162, 486, 1,458; Rule: ×3

Commutative Property 55
1. C, G, H
2. D, I
3. A. correct B. correct C. no
   D. no E. correct F. correct
   G. no H. no I. 3 + 2 = 2 + 3

Associative Property 56
1. no; no
2. yes; yes
3. Jenna's is correct. Crystal made a mistake.

Associative Property 57
1. yes; examples may vary
2. no; examples may vary
3. yes; examples may vary

Function Tables 58
1. yes
2. Check students work.
3. yes; (11, 24) should be (37, 24)

Function Tables 59
1.
| IN: | 2 | 9 | 81 | 76 | 37 | 25 | 42 |
| OUT: | 11 | 18 | 90 | 85 | 46 | 34 | 51 |

Rule: OUT = IN + 9

2.
| IN: | 82 | 16 | 70 | 34 | 44 | 50 | 60 |
| OUT: | 41 | 8 | 35 | 17 | 22 | 25 | 30 |

Rule: OUT = IN ÷ 2

3.
| IN: | 7 | 20 | 8 | 3 | 41 | 5 | 6 |
| OUT: | 21 | 60 | 24 | 9 | 123 | 15 | 18 |

Rule: OUT = IN × 3

4.
| IN: | 52 | 73 | 18 | 20 | 35 | 91 | 88 |
| OUT: | 37 | 58 | 3 | 5 | 20 | 76 | 73 |

Rule: OUT = IN − 15

Variables 60
1. $m = 26$ 7. $c = 3$
2. correct 8. $n = 6$
3. correct 9. correct
4. $u = 4$
5. correct
6. $e = 40$

Variables 61
1. $m = 26$ 6. $e = 59$
2. $s = 76$ 7. $a = 7$
3. $t = 12$ 8. $d = 3$
4. $u = 8$ 9. $g = 19$
5. $b = 18$ 10. $j = 14$

Variables 62
1. 2 × 7 = 14? yes; 2 − 7 = 5? no
2. Tremaine should have switched the answers. (spider) = 7 and (flower) = 2
3. (sun) = 6 and (star) = 8
4. (triangle) = 6 and (square) = 2

Variables 63
1. (triangle) = 7; (square) = 8
2. (trapezoid) = 5; (rectangle) = 4
3. (hexagon) = 15; (pentagon) = 11
4. (circle) = 8; (parallelogram) = 4
5. (octagon) = 6; (diamond) = 2

Applications—Writing Equations 64
1. $V = 2 \times 12 = 24$
2. no
3. $C = 2 \times V$
4. 6; yes
5. 20; yes

Applications—Writing Equations 65
1. $C + S = 24$
2. $O = 5 + L$
3. $B = M - 7$
4. $R = 3 \times T$

Applications—Writing Equations 66
1. yes
2. yes; ? miles to the store + 7 miles to the mall = a total of 18 miles
3. yes; 11 + 7 = 18

© McGraw-Hill Children's Publishing

0-7424-2783-8 *Is That Correct?*

Answer Key

Applications—Writing Equations 67
1. A. $s = 12 + m$
   B. $45 = 12 + m$; $m = 33$
2. A. $t = 5 + w$
   B. $8 = 5 + w$; $w = 3$
3. A. $a + c = 9$
   B. $5 + c = 9$; $c = 4$

Applications—Graphing 68
1. yes
2. $8 weeks 1-2; $6 weeks 2-3; $5 weeks 3-4; $6 weeks 4-5
3. no; He saved the most between weeks 1 and 2 and the least between weeks 3 and 4.
4. For the "Amount Saved," Luke did not go up by the same amount each time. He used the data values instead of an even scale.

Applications—Graphing 69
1. different amounts
2. most: $7 between weeks 2 and 3; least: $2 between weeks 0 and 1

Similar and Congruent 70
1. A. similar; B. congruent; C. neither
2. congruent
3. neither
4. similar

Similar and Congruent 71
1. similar   2. neither   3. similar
4. congruent 5. congruent 6. similar
7. neither   8. congruent 9. neither

Symmetry 72
1. yes
2. yes; There are 3 more through the corners between points.
3. 6
4. 5; from each vertex to the midpoint of the opposite side
5. 6; between opposite vertices and between midpoints of opposite sides
6. 3; from each vertex to the midpoint of the opposite side

Symmetry 73
1. correct
2. incorrect
3. correct
4. incorrect
5. correct
6. incorrect
7. incorrect
8. correct
9. correct

Reflections and Rotations 74
1. A
2. B

Reflections and Rotations 75
1. rotation   4. rotation
2. reflection 5. rotation
3. reflection 6. reflection

Types of Triangles 76
1. 3
2. 2
3. 0
4. no; A should be isosceles.

Types of Triangles 77
1. isosceles
2. isosceles
3. scalene
4. equilateral
5. scalene
6. scalene

Polygons 78
1. Answers may vary.
2. A: yes; yes; yes
   B: yes; yes; yes
   C: yes; yes; no
3. A and B

Polygons 79
1. polygon
2. not a polygon
3. not a polygon
4. polygon
5. polygon
6. not a polygon
7. not a polygon
8. polygon
9. not a polygon

3-Dimensional Shapes 80
1. yes
2. no
3. no
4. no
5. B

3-Dimensional Shapes 81
1. hexagonal prism
2. rectangular pyramid
3. rectangular prism
4. triangular prism

Applications—Point of View 82
1. yes
2. yes
3. no; The right side view should be 3 cubes high.
4. Top Front Right

Applications—Nets 83
1. no
2. Cube C is correct.
3. B

Applications—Using a Grid 84
1. Chad: yes; yes; no
   Todd: yes; yes; yes
   Jeff: no; no yes
2. Todd

Applications—Using a Grid 85
1. 5 miles
2. 10 miles
3. 17 miles
4. 15 miles

Applications—Coordinate Graphing 86
1. correct
2. (5, 6)
3. correct
4. correct
5. (5, 2)
6. (4, 4)
7. correct
8. (8, 1)

Applications—Coordinate Graphing 87
1. (2, 3)   7. (5, 7)
2. (3, 3)   8. (0, 4)
3. (5, 4)   9. (2, 6)
4. (3, 5)   10. (1, 7)
5. (6, 1)   11. (1, 4)
6. (4, 2)   12. (6, 6)

Area and Perimeter 88
1. yes; yes
2. Answers may vary.
3. yes; yes
4. Rosa is wrong. She assumed that two rectangles with the same perimeter would be the same shape. She didn't take into account the case where two different rectangles have the same perimeter. Nina showed that two different rectangles with the same perimeter can have different areas. One counterexample is all it takes to prove a statement false.

© McGraw-Hill Children's Publishing

0-7424-2783-8 *Is That Correct?*

Answer Key

Area and Perimeter 89
1. true
2. false; area will be 4x larger
3. false; A 3 x 4 rectangle has a perimeter of 14 but a 2 x 6 rectangle has a perimeter of 16.

Volume 90
1. 24
2. 3
3. 72
4. yes
5. 32 cu. ft.

Volume 91
1. 120 cu. in.
2. 96 cu. in.
3. 96 cu. in.
4. 56 cu. in.
5. 42 cu. in.
6. 64 cu. in.

Customary Units 92
1. capacity
2. Taylor's
3. cups
4. gallons

Customary Units 93
1. C
2. J
3. M
4. I
5. D or K
6. G
7. F
8. A
9. H
10. E

Metric Units 94
1. mass
2. Alfonso's and Matteo's
3. grams
4. kilograms

Metric Units 95
1. G
2. D
3. C
4. A
5. I
6. F
7. E
8. H
9. B

Converting Customary Lengths 96
1. 21 ft.
2. correct
3. 2 yd.
4. correct
5. correct
6. correct
7. 36 inches
8. correct
9. 10,560 ft.
10. $\frac{1}{3}$ ft.

Converting Customary Lengths 97
1. 3 ft.
2. 30 ft.
3. 21,120 ft.
4. 96 in.
5. 22 yd.
6. 3 mi.
7. 120 in.
8. 36 ft.
9. 4 yd.
10. 10,560 ft.
11. 9 ft.
12. 1 ft.

Converting Metric Lengths 98
1. 2,000 cm
2. correct
3. correct
4. 320 cm
5. correct
6. 4,000 mm
7. correct
8. 50,000 m

Converting Metric Lengths 99
1. 4,000 cm
2. 2,000 m
3. 8 m
4. 532 cm
5. 6,200 cm
6. 7,000 mm
7. 20 cm
8. 80,000 m
9. 600 cm
10. 9 m
11. 500 cm
12. 80 mm

Applications—Money 100
1. yes
2. 17; no
3. no
4. Carmen and Manuela
5. Possible Answer: 7 dimes
6. 10 nickels

Applications—Money 101
1. Both boys received the same dollar value.
2. No; the same number of pieces doesn't mean the amount is the same.
3. Possible Answer: Thaniel: 2 one-dollar bills and 2 dimes; Ty: 1 one-dollar bill, 3 quarters, 3 dimes, and 3 nickels
4. Possible Answer: Loen: 2 one-dollar bills and 1 quarter; Shawn: 1 one-dollar bill, 1 half dollar, 2 quarters, 2 dimes, and 1 nickel
5. Possible Answer: Rashon: 3 one-dollar bills, 3 quarters, 1 dime, and 1 nickel; Kordell: 2 one-dollar bills, 4 quarters, 4 dimes, and 1 half dollar.

Applications—Time 102
1. 12:25
2. 1:00
3. yes
4. 30 minutes
5. 20 minutes

Applications—Time 103
1. Check students' drawings.
2. Check students' drawings.
3. 10 minutes
4. no; Patrick will be 5 minutes late.
5. 7:50 A.M.
6. 7:50 P.M.

Applications—Temperature 104
1. higer
2. no; The Fahrenheit temperature should be higher than 30.
3. 90°F
4. Answers may vary.

Applications—Temperature 105
1. 70°F
2. swimming; 84°F
3. 25°C
4. 5°C

How Likely? 106
1. Answers may vary.
2. You must be at least 18 to play the lotto. Armando is too young to play, so he couldn't possibly win. But, Armando could know an adult who could play and possibly win, even though the chances are slim.
3. The weather will be different in different locations. One boy may live in a rainy area, and the other in a dry area.
4. Armando answered the question on a Friday. Since there is no school on Saturday, he is certain all the students will be absent the next day. Enrique answered the questions 3 days later, on a Monday. It's unlikely that all the students would be absent on Tuesday.
5. yes; If the person lived in Mexico, Independence Day would be celebrated in May.

Equally Likely 107
1. 3; 3; yes
2. yes
3. 3; 2; no
4. 2; 3; no
5. 2; 2; yes
6. no; D is also correct

Equally Likely 108
1. yes
2. no
3. Half the area of the spinner has an outcome of 3. Only a quarter of the spinner has an outcome of 1 or 2. So, the spinner is most likely to land on 3.
4. The outcomes of 1 and 2 are equally likely, since they take up the same amount of space on the spinner.
5. yes
6. no
7. yes

Probability 109
1. denominator; Hareem's and Kenton's
2. 2; 4; no
3. 1; 6; yes
4. Jeffon
5. Carnell put the number of cubes of that color in the numerator. He put the number of remaining cubes in the denominator. He should have put the total number of cubes in the denominator.

© McGraw-Hill Children's Publishing

0-7424-2783-8 *Is That Correct?*

Answer Key

Probability 110
1. 1 and 6; 6 and 1; 2 and 5; 5 and 2; 3 and 4; 4 and 3; 6 ways
2. $\frac{6}{36}$
3. 3 and 6; 6 and 3; 4 and 5; 5 and 4; 4 ways
4. $\frac{4}{36}$
5. no; Anica has a better chance of rolling a 7 then Carlota does of rolling a 9.

Probability 111
1. $\frac{4}{8}$
2. $\frac{1}{8}$
3. $\frac{1}{8}$
4. $\frac{4}{8}$
5. $\frac{2}{8}$
6. $\frac{2}{6}$
7. $\frac{2}{6}$
8. $\frac{2}{6}$
9. $\frac{1}{6}$
10. $\frac{3}{6}$

Range 112
1. yes
2. no; range will be different
3. Mrs. Rodriguez: correct
   Mr. Mohammed: min = 2; max = 6; range = 4
   Ms. Chin: min = 0, max = 8; range = 8
   Miss Rogers: min = 0; max = 7; range = 7

Mode 113
1. Benito
2. yes
3. Mrs. Rodriguez: 1; Mr. Mohammed: 3; Ms. Chin: 2

Median 114
1. Aidan
2. yes
3. Mrs. Rodriguez: 3; Mr. Mohammed: 4; Ms. Chin: 3.5

Mean 115
1. Anh
2. yes
3. Mrs. Rodriguez: 3.7; Mr. Mohammed: 3.9; Ms. Chin: 3.8

Applications—Interpreting Data 116
1. range = 9
2. mean = 26
3. median = 25
4. mode = 24

Applications—Interpreting Data 117
1. mode = 12
2. mean = 11
3. range = 11
4. median = 11

Applications—Tally Charts 118
1. 5 items
2. count by 5's
3. count each mark as 1
4. Monday: correct
   Tuesday: 16
   Wednesday: correct
   Thursday: 14
   Friday: correct

Applications—Tally Charts 119
1. squirrel
2. bird; 16
3. goose; 6
4. 9
5. 15

Applications—Line Plots 120
1.
Days	Mon.	Tues.	Wed.	Thur.	Fri.	Sat.	Sun.
Cust.	40	70	70	100	120	180	190

2. Mon.-Tues = 30; Tues.-Wed. = 0; Wed.-Thur. = 30 Thur.-Fri. = 20; Fri.-Sat. = 60; Sat.-Sun. = 10
3. most = Fri.-Sat.; least = Sat.-Sun.; none = Tues.-Wed.

Applications—Bar Graphs 121
1. Place the ruler horizontally along the top of the bar. See what number it touches on the scale.
2. The bar represents the number halfway between the two numbers on the scale.
3. basketball = 19; baseball = 11; football = 8; soccer = 22; volleyball = 14
4. A. correct; B. correct; C. 3; D. 3

Applications—Bar Graphs 122
1. 8
2. 2
3. bus and walking
4. Both distances are the same.
5. No; There should be a greater distance between 12 and 20 than there is between 10 and 12. The numbers on the scale should go up by the same amount each time.